HomeRecording
STUDIO BASICS

Authors:
Jon Chappell, Rusty Cutchin, David Darlington, Pat Kirtley, Mike Levine, Julian McBrowne,
Emile Menasché, Levin Pfeufer, Bill Philbrick, Arty Skye, Jerry Tardif

Cherry Lane Music Company
Educational Director/Project Supervisor: Susan Poliniak
Director of Publications: Mark Phillips
Publications Coordinator: Rebecca Skidmore

ISBN 978-1-60378-323-1

Visit our website at www.cherrylaneprint.com

Table of Contents

Studio Setup and Sound Conditioning

Cables and Connectors

Gear—Selection and Issues

Monitors and Monitoring

Recording

Effects

Mixers, Mixing, and Mastering

Studio Setup and Sound Conditioning

The Sweet Spot
How to Turn That Sow's Ear of a Workspace into a Silk Purse
By Rusty Cutchin

It's a design truism that "form follows function." Even if, like me, you've spent most of your life wondering what the hell that means while searching for the perfect groove, guitar sound, or sample, at some point you'll find yourself thinking about what your studio looks like and how this affects the quality of your work. "Form follows function" (think of them as the "F words" of design) simply means that the *look* of something is less important than how the thing *works*. "Duh," you're thinking, "Can I get back to work now?"

We all know that the quality of the audio work is the most important aspect of your studio, but it's wise not to underestimate the positive results of a room that looks (and functions) great. With the explosion of home recording around the world, there are an amazing number of affordable (or free) options available to the person who wants to organize and stylize his or her studio. Almost overnight, you can transform yourself into a studio *fashionista* and leave behind the guy who looks around his room and wonders, "Now, where *did* I put that mixing board?"

Rules of the Room

Of course, good design and organization come naturally to some people. Pro studios have to make it a priority because of competition, and therein lies the first rule you should remember about the layout of your own studio.

Rule 1: People Like to Work in a Clean, Organized Workspace

And that's not just because it looks good. In a well-designed studio, people have plenty of room to spread out, they don't become fatigued as quickly, and the work ultimately goes faster. When your tools are organized ("Why, of course, that patch cable's right here, along with my 400 other neatly-arranged-by-length patch cables"), clients feel that they're working with a guy who gets the job done, even if you walk upstairs to the household-from-hell after the session.

Now, you have to understand that the idea of me writing about workspace organization is like Mike Tyson writing about brain surgery. Except for the fact that he may eventually need some, he's spectacularly unqualified. People who know me feel that I have similar qualifications regarding organization. Nevertheless, a studio is not a desk covered with press releases, newspapers, software boxes, CDs, and photos of Shania Twain. And this suggests a second rule.

Rule 2: Keep Your Messes Organized and Out of Sight

If you tend to put off chores such as straightening up, then ensure that the studio is cleaned up *first*. Sure, one of the great attractions of a home studio is working the way *you* want to work and not letting anything get in the way of the music—not even pet hair in the patchbays or Coke in the console (both of which, I'm ashamed to say, I had to deal with in my early studio days). But even if you don't want to live in a sterile, Martha Stewart–type house, you will grow to prefer a studio that looks as if she set it up. You may not mind searching through piles of pizza boxes to find that track sheet, but the people you want to produce will.

I began recording and producing in Texas and moved to New York after I'd been in the business for several years. The biggest adjustment I had to make (besides replacing Mexican food with Italian) was the *spatial* adjustment. Learning to operate in smaller and more vertical spaces is one of the primary challenges a studio owner faces in urban areas. And what kind of space in a studio is the most critical (just as in any room of the house)? *Floor space*. Thus, rule three.

Rule 3: Keep Your Stuff off the Floor

It's only natural when you run out of wall space to requisition the nearest surface for extra stuff such as computer printers, road cases, cables, shoes, pizza boxes, etc.—and the nearest surface is almost always the floor. But using it for storage is a mistake. Nothing makes a room feel more crowded and cramped than extra stuff spread out around the floor or under the desk. It's also unnecessary, particularly if the items are mostly unused and, as in many big-city apartments, the room has high ceilings, which means lots of unused wall space. Figure out how to use that wall space or find a closet or seldom-used room in which to stash things—anything that you don't need on a daily basis. I've been in New York home studios that would feel twice as big if all of the unnecessary stuff was off the floor.

Arranging and Conducting ... the Furniture

Once you recognize the need for clean space and get all of the unnecessary stuff out of your studio, you're getting close to the fun part, which is spending money to set up or replace the fundamental pieces in the room. No, this isn't the gear—it's the stuff that *holds* the gear (and holds the people, for that matter). With so many good-looking and functional pieces of furniture and storage units out there, you should never have to rely on a rickety keyboard stand to hold your mixer, or your hippie uncle's musty beanbag chair for the clients.

By the way, right now is a good time to consider taking care of any structural problems in the room: sound containment issues, monitoring problems, etc.

If you know that the room is ready to go sonically, then consider the following rules when you're moving in furniture, gear racks, stands, and storage units.

Place the Longest Unit on the Shortest Wall

This is an old rule of furniture arranging that often comes as a revelation to people setting up a home for the first time—it creates more apparent floor space. It should actually be fairly intuitive to a studio designer, because the "longest" unit will almost always be the mixing console/monitor arrangement. If the monitors are arranged on the shortest wall, there will be more airspace between them and the rear wall, which will help you deal with reflections easier and generally make the room sound better with less work. It will also afford more room between you, the monitors, and the other people in the room.

Why does this layout seem like the opposite of that in pro control rooms? Simple—they are bigger rooms, in general, and they have more resources to deal with acoustic problems.

Think Horizontally for Working, Vertically for Storing

I'm always amazed at the energy of engineers in small-space studios who love jumping up and down to fix something—a glitchy banana plug behind a power amp on the floor or a DIP switch on the MIDI interface at the top of an 8' rack. Come on! I say, if you can't reach it from an office chair, it ain't worth tweakin'! What may sound like a strategy born out of laziness will help in conserving energy that may be needed when things go wrong and a session lasts longer than expected (and just like with money, every little bit adds up). Even in a small room, it's easy to lay out your work surface and primary gear horizontally. One way to do this is by using affordable and widely available furniture such as computer workstations, even if you don't use a computer in your studio.

Likewise, if you must store all of your peripheral gear in the studio, make use of all of the room's available height with bookcases, cabinets (preferably with doors), or other shelving. Often, other storage units can be placed on the top shelf for leftover items. They can also be placed in closets to take advantage of the unused vertical space.

Measure Twice, Buy Once

Sometimes there's a built-in problem that must be dealt with. Maybe in your studio, the vocal booth is also the laundry room, or maybe you don't have enough clearance between the door and the side wall for that great couch you wanted.

Get over it! There's more than one way to skin a cat or cut a track. The perfect studio layout sometimes requires patience and planning. Not enough room for the mixing station you were going to buy or build? Can't install that perfect rack because it will block the window? Relax, step back, and consider alternatives.

A home studio can be as expensive and beautiful or as inexpensive and funky as you want it to be. The important thing is that it makes you feel good working in it, and that it makes you want to come back. (Just keep the stuff off the floor, *aaaiight?*)

Supply-Side Recording
Cheap Studio Upgrades
By David Darlington

In studio life as in real life, it's the little things that matter. Sometimes the smallest detail can be the difference between music-making heaven and, well, somewhere else. Recently I looked around my composing studio and made a list of several little items that more than once have saved the day and the session. Here are some of my faves.

1 *Artist Tape and Sharpies*

Labels are your friends. I use white artist tape with light-tack adhesive that's easy to apply to a mixer in order to label tracks. It's easy to pull it off when I'm done, and it doesn't leave a residue. I like to color-coordinate my channel labels so that I can easily get a visual reference of what's going on—blue for drums, red for vocals, green for keys, etc. You'd be surprised how this helps your train of thought while composing or mixing. You won't waste time wondering what's on Track 12 and whether or not it's important.

2 *Ground Lift Adapters and Power Strips*

There is never enough juice in a studio. When your guitar player brings in that super phaser from 1975, have a ready place for him to plug it in. Then, when it's buzzing like a chainsaw, lift the ground with those common, gray, three-prong-to-two-prong adapters. I keep a bunch in the toolbox.

3 *Computer Printer (or Typewriter)*

A printed label for your CD immediately tells clients that you are in business, and not just playing around with a hobby. It may take a few tries to get the computer to spit out a decent label, but once you've got it, save it as a template. A small investment here can pay big dividends.

4 *Portable Radio (Boom Box) with Line Inputs*

Plug your mixer into this and play that mix you've just approved. Sounds a bit different from what you just listened to on those Rump Shaker 5000 speakers that cost an arm and a leg, doesn't it? Now ask yourself which system most music consumers will have when listening to your stuff. My guess is it's the el cheapo boom box. Make your mix adjustments and then listen again on the Rump Shakers. You'll probably find that the adjustments actually *improved* your mix!

5 Soft Lighting

Most of the time, I like to see what's going on in the room, so I keep the room lights up to maintain a no-nonsense working environment. But often in the later stages of mixing it's a good idea to take your eyes out of the mixing process. Turn off the overhead light and just leave on the lava lamp. This will help you concentrate on the feel of the music and assess its visceral impact.

6 Coasters

Not the oldies group, but the little things you put drinks on. Actually, I like those furniture cubes you can get at the unfinished furniture store. They keep drinks, food, and even ashtrays below the height of the gear. This minimizes the possibility (and aftermath) of a mishap. Keeping liquid away from electronics may seem obvious, but I know techs who make a living by cleaning Diet Coke out of recording gear. A slick trick is to cut holes into the tops of the cubes—you can set the cups down into them so they can't spill.

7 Documentation Sheets

I find it useful to have diagrams of some of my outboard gear to document how it was used on a session or a mix. Most processors have user storage in their software, but it's also important to know the input and output levels, and how the gear was connected. Make a drawing of each piece (or copy the diagram in the manual) with data fields for the internal parameters, and keep a master file of your entire studio. Make copies (or computer printouts) of a "session recall" package, which includes everything from a particular session. Then, if you have to come back to a mix or record the same vocalist much later, you can remember what was going on.

8 Acoustic Foam

If you're just starting out in a basic home situation, you can use a few pieces of foam on the walls to tone down reflections. Good places to start are midway between your speakers on the wall you face while listening, and in the center of the wall directly behind you. Experiment by moving them around a bit. The idea is to make the room sound the same no matter where the listener is positioned.

9 Patchbay

When you're in a position to upgrade your studio from basic to mid-line, the place to start is with a patchbay, which can be purchased at any music store and installed yourself. With just a little planning, you can vastly improve the flexibility of your setup.

10 | *Comfortable Chair*

You may argue that this is not studio equipment, but I beg to differ. Think about how many hours a day you use your vocal mic and what you spent for it. Now, assess how many hours a day your butt is in that chair and how much you shelled out for it! See my point? Don't be chintzy when it comes to your chair, and your neck and spine will thank you for it. Oh, yeah—your mixes will sound better, too.

Adventures in Airspace
Making the Most of Your Listening Environment
By David Darlington

If you are constructing a studio control room in your home, you've probably spent a lot of time deciding on your equipment purchases—your choice of speakers and mixing board and other such considerations. Basically, you set it all on a table or keyboard stand, fired it up, and it sounded great, right? If you did your homework, it did, but even when your sound is awesome, truly effective studios are more than meets the ears. Music can fly off your desktop in any kind of room, but if you spend a little thought and a few bucks on your control room environment, you can significantly improve the quality of your listening space and, often, your music.

Surface Considerations

The first thing to consider is the shape of the space itself. Is your room large or small? Wide or narrow? Try to find a place for your speakers that allows ample room in front for the sound to develop outward, but not so large that it creates unwanted echoes. If you're in a basement or large rec room, consider making the space smaller with some sort of divider—one that absorbs or disperses sound instead of creating reflections. If your space is small, place the speakers along the long wall and give them enough separation to create a good stereo field, but avoid corners that trap bass frequencies and make speakers sound boomy. Also, keep your speakers a foot or two away from the back wall to avoid reflections.

The next consideration is the texture of your wall surfaces. Basically, a "true" sounding control room is made up of many different kinds of textures: *reflective* (hard walls), *absorbent* (carpets and curtains), and *refractive* (shelves and bookcases). The floor is often the best place to start (before the gear comes in). A cement or wood floor usually needs some type of carpet to stop reflections; choose a rug with a thickness that won't make the floor too "dead." I like to have a bit of hard surface on the floor, preferably just in front of the mixer, so I will often lay a throw rug behind the listening position, leaving the floor in front of the mixer exposed. There should also be carpet along the front wall and under the mixer table to control reflections from the surfaces nearest the monitors. Remember: A lot of traffic may tread there, so go with the highest quality carpeting you can afford.

Ceilings are a bit more difficult to change, so you might just have to make the best of what you have. If you have handyman skills and your ceiling is made of a very hard surface such as cement, you're better off installing a drop ceiling of acoustic tiles. The parts for this type of ceiling are readily available at home-improvement centers. They consist of an aluminum grid frame that suspends from hangers that you install into the ceiling, and acoustic tiles that are "dropped" into the squares of the grid. This creates a semi-absorbent surface. To further deaden the ceiling, you can add insulation above the tiles. If you are really adept at this sort of thing, angle the ceiling down slightly towards the listener and then back up as the new ceiling approaches the rear wall. Remember that you're trying to avoid parallel surfaces. This angled ceiling also looks great, and it really impresses the clients!

If you can't drop the ceiling because of space limitations, the next best treatment is to break the surface with light fixtures, textured paint, or anything that will keep sound waves from reflecting in a pattern. The goal is to break up the wave and diffuse it into many smaller waves that won't color the sound in your listening position.

Panel Discussion

Hard walls are usually treated with a combination of *absorbers* (soft surfaces) and *diffusers* (multifaceted reflective surfaces). You can create these kinds of surfaces easily and inexpensively with supplies from a home store.

One of the easiest pieces to build is an absorber. Basically, this piece is just a large picture-frame construction filled with insulation and then covered with stretch fabric and hung on the wall. First, determine how much of the wall you want covered. Walk around the room clapping your hands and listen for very quick echoes, called *early reflections*. Hang absorbers on the walls that produce the loudest of these reflections.

Cut a piece of 3/4" plywood to the shape you need. About 4'x8' is okay, but your walls may require 2'x8' or 4'x4'. Tailor the shape to cover a large portion of the offending wall. Next, nail thin wood strips (2"x1/2") around the edge and flush with the back of the plywood, creating a frame. Inside this frame, staple yellow fiberglass insulation such as the kind used around air conditioning ducts. Completely fill the frame.

Buy some inexpensive stretchy fabric in the color of your studio decor. I usually go with basic black, but if fuscia is your thing, go for it! Staple the fabric to the outside edge of the top of the frame and then stretch it downward and staple it firmly to the outside bottom edge of the frame. Stretch it again to staple the side edges. You now have a large cloth-covered frame with unsightly staples and ragged cloth on the outside edges. Simply trim the cloth and layer another strip of 2"x1/2" wood around the outside edge and paint the edges to match the decor. Lastly, use molding to make an edge around the front to create a picture frame. If you are a decent carpenter, miter the corners at a 45-degree angle. Don't forget to paint these surfaces first so you don't ruin the cloth. Now, just attach this whole assembly to the wall with hooks and fasteners, and voilà! Sonic treatment worthy of the Museum of Modern Art! Be creative with the sizes and shapes for best results. I even have an inverted U-shape around my control room window that really tones down my front wall and looks very high-tech.

Getting Cornered

In certain parts of your room, your clapping test will produce more of a tone or ring than an actual echo. These obnoxious sounds are called *standing waves* and they're hard to kill. They often appear in corners where two large, hard surfaces meet, such as ceiling corners. One way to treat these is with a combination absorber/diffuser. The basic material for this is pegboard—just like the kind you use in a garage for hanging power tools. Cut a length of pegboard to fit your problem area. These shapes do not necessarily have to be oblong; in fact, it's better if they're not. Use unusual angles and V-shapes for the best results. Get the same type of fabric you used on the absorbers and stretch it around the shape like wrapping paper. Staple the fabric to the back surface so the staples won't show. The trick to successfully using these pieces is hanging them at an angle between the two adjoining surfaces. For example, if you're trying to solve a problem in the corner of the ceiling, fix the piece to the wall at its lower edge, and then let the top protrude forward using picture-frame wire so that it hangs away from the ceiling at a 45-degree angle. When sound heads for the corner, some will be reflected and some will pass through the tiny holes in the pegboard. The waves that pass through the holes will strike the ceiling and wall at odd angles and be diffused in many different directions. Result: no more standing wave. These weird shapes hanging at odd angles from high on the walls also make great conversation pieces and demonstrate to your guests your vast knowledge of acoustics and physics!

Up Against the Wall

Finally, you'll need to treat the rear wall, which causes the majority of reflected sound to come back to your listening position and distort your sonic image. The piece you want to hang on the rear wall is a diffuser and it is also based on the picture-frame motif. This shape is usually oblong and wider than it is high.

A good size to start with is 4'x8', because plywood is sold in that size. This time, make your edges from stronger wood strips (e.g., 1"x2") since they will be adding needed support. Fill the basic frame with carpet (color coordinated, of course). Yes, I know carpet is absorbent, but first you need to tone down the parallel surface.

Next, cut lots of slats, about 1-1/2"x1/4". These will lie vertically in the frame; they need to be long enough to reach from inside the frame at the top to outside the frame at the bottom, creating a slight downward tilt. The next adjacent strip goes inside at the bottom to outside at the top, creating an opposite upward tilt. Keep layering adjacent strips to fill the whole frame, making a pattern of upward and downward angles. Sound waves that hit these strips will be broken up and reflected in many different directions, diffusing the sound.

Finish off the frame with a border of molding, mitered at the corners, and paint all of the wood to match your decor. Affix the diffuser solidly to the back wall in the center behind the listening position to effectively neutralize the wall.

There are other ways to break up large, parallel surfaces. Bookcases with lots of different-sized books make great natural diffusers. If you have cabinets in the room, try hanging doors that are a bit too large, so that when they close, the doors create a slight outward angle. Also try putting foam or carpet swatches on the cabinet doors to cut down on reflections.

So, in summary, there are three principles to keep in mind.

1. Avoid parallel surfaces. Wherever they exist, create angles and/or break up the surfaces.

2. Use a combination of hard and soft surfaces in a room to create a natural listening environment that is neither overly live nor dead.

3. Don't spend a ton of money on products that you can create yourself.

Filling in the Cracks
If You Really Want to Contain Sound from Room to Room,
You Must Seal the Deal
By Arty Skye

Before I built my own studio, I studied studio design techniques and noticed a wide discrepancy in the way professional studios, many of which I work in regularly, were built. I remember a session in a world-class studio with completely redesigned and recently remodeled rooms. It looked great, the control room was true (for the most part), and the whole vibe of the studio felt very comfortable. I also noticed that the wall dividing the control room and the studio was about 3' thick, with the usual rectangular window installed within.

While the clients were listening to the mix, I decided to wander around the newly designed live room. I walked into a side room used for vocal overdubs and out its back exit, shutting the doors behind me, to enter the live room. *Hmmm*, I thought sarcastically, *nice isolation*—when I heard the Yamaha NS-10 monitors bleeding loudly through the glass between the rooms.

With a 3' wall, it made no sense that the NS-10s were audible. These are, after all, near-field, bookshelf speakers and not giant primary reference monitors. I examined the way the glass was fitted into the window (it was actually two windows, one mounted on each side of the wall) and realized why the seal wasn't working. The glass was attached directly to the wood with a bead of silicone sealant around the baseline. The same was true for the sheet of glass on the other side of the wall. I had seen this design many times before, but never had a reason to question it until now. This technique didn't make sense because the vibrations would transfer from the wall to the glass and back. The 3' wall basically had a huge hole in it, which made it quite ineffective.

Another problem was apparent in the door seals, or lack of them. Although the studio had installed thick wood doors, they were left with about a 1/2" gap at the bottom. They were like regular doors that you see in a house, with no sound-isolating material around the threshold. These fundamental isolation problems had been overlooked in the construction of this multi–million-dollar studio (which otherwise is one of my favorite studios in New York).

The Real Deal on Seals

When I was designing my studio, I picked up a book called *How to Build a Small Budget Recording Studio from Scratch* by Alton F. Everest, and Michael Shea. One of the authors, Mike Shea, happened to be a former teacher of mine at New York's Institute of Audio Research (IAR). He agreed to come down to my studio before construction and give me some advice, which turned out to be invaluable. Mike gave me a rundown on the proper way to install internal windows. The secret to success lies in mounting the glass properly.

Many people working in a commercial recording studio for the first time notice that the panes of glass in a control room window are angled. There are two reasons for this: The first is to control reflections. When the glass is straight, reflections bounce back and forth between the two panes—you sacrifice the integrity of the seal, get standing waves, and end up with a completely reflective surface inside both rooms. The second is to avoid the mirror effect (which lures musicians into looking at themselves when they should be watching the engineer!), which can be quite distracting. Whether or not you decide to angle your windows, it's relatively easy to seal them effectively and professionally.

Step-by-Step Through the Looking Glass

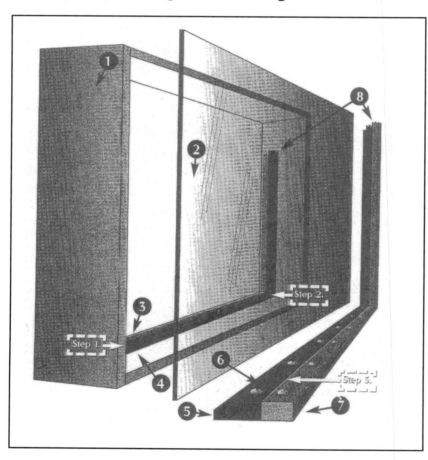

1. Wood frame inside wall
2. Glass pane
3. Molding "stop"
4. Neoprene rubber seal for front of pane
5. Neoprene rubber seal for edge of pane
6. Neoprene rubber seal for back of pane
7. Molding "stop"
8. Molding and neoprene continue around perimeter

To prepare a window area for sealing, first you need to frame the inside of the window with wood. Use a level and make sure the surfaces are smooth and even. Use clear silicone to fill in any gaps in the wood.

1. You'll need some wood molding, about 3/4" high; I used 1" square molding, but you can also use 1/4" rounds. Frame the inside of the window space, creating a vertical angle outward at the top (ten degrees is sufficient), if possible. Make sure to leave enough room for the thickness of the glass plus another piece of molding. Add in the thickness of the insulating material (I use neoprene) and double it. For example, if your wall is 1" thick and you're using 1/2" thick glass, you want the top (if it's angled) of the inside frame to be no less than 2-1/4" from the edge: 3/4" molding, plus 1/2" neoprene, plus 1/2"-thick glass, plus 1/2" neoprene, equals 2-1/4".

2. Buy 1/2" thick by 1/2"- to 3/4"-wide closed-cell neoprene rubber with an adhesive backing. Measure the entire perimeter of the window and multiply by seven—this will give you the total length of rubber you need for both panes (you're going to surround each pane three times, and multiplying by seven gives you enough for back-up). Now, you need to know how thick the glass on this side is going to be. It's best to use two different thicknesses, such as 1/2" and 5/8", so that they won't have the same resonant frequency. You'll be cutting neoprene for the edges of the glass. The idea here is to totally sandwich, or float, the glass between the rubber so that the glass is isolated from the wood.

3. Take the neoprene and run it along the outside of the molding facing you. Make it neat and tight. Next, take the neoprene of the same width as the glass and run it along the wood frame at right angles to and butted up tightly against the neoprene you previously put down. The glass will rest on this rubber. You'll probably need to maneuver the glass a bit to fit it into this rubber frame. Next, you'll have some previously cut molding to match the same lengths as the molding you just used to frame the glass. Carefully attach neoprene to this molding and screw the molding into place, butted up tightly against the glass. Repeat the procedure for the other piece of glass.

Here are a few tips that can help you with the installation.

-   Make sure that you clean the glass thoroughly before mounting it. Fingerprints or smudges on the inside of the glass will drive you crazy.

-   If you're staining the molding, make sure you do so before you start attaching the neoprene.

-   If you want a felt look inside the window, one inexpensive and easy way to do this is to get some Styrofoam board, cut it to the dimensions that you need (usually the space between the two pieces of molding), and wrap the felt around it. You can use adhesive spray to make the felt hold fast to the Styrofoam board. Frame the inside of the window with it, but make sure that it's attached properly on all sides–you don't want the top sagging in the middle six months later. Use screws to attach the molding to the window frame. This way, if you need to get in there for any reason, or if a mic stand goes through the window and you need to replace the glass, it's much easier to remove than if it was glued on or attached with nails.

Door Seals

The cheap and easy way is to get some more of that closed-cell neoprene and put it around the threshold of your door. A better way is to remove the existing molding from around the inside of the door and replace it with thicker 1" square molding. Put some thick neoprene around the inside of this with enough clearance to close the door with a gentle push, compressing the neoprene slightly and creating a snug fit.

A more expensive but better way is to contact a company called Zero International (*www.zerointernational.com*), which makes great seals for doors. Besides the rubber for around the sides, they also have a bar for the bottom of the door. When the door is closed, this bar lowers automatically, pressing the rubber to the floor and completing the seal.

Build Your Own Studio Baffles
How to Fight Reflections and Win
By Jerry Tardif

Home studios can be found in all types of spaces. Attics, basements, living rooms, dining rooms, and bedrooms are all possibilities for use as recording areas. The problem is that none of these spaces were specifically designed for recording, so they're likely to have physical features that present acoustical problems due to the way that sound reflects in them. You can control sonic reflections with the strategic placement of baffles, which you can build yourself at a low cost. Dealing with reflections is very much like mic placement—part science, part art. Once you understand the basics, you can experiment until you find the solutions that work for you.

Everything in a room affects sound. Hard surfaces reflect it, soft ones absorb it. Some larger rooms seem to have just the right amount of each and sound great with little or no treatment. In fact, many people will work hard trying to create that "perfect" recording space with just the "right" acoustics. But for most home studios, it makes more sense to deaden the main room and add reverberation through a controlled space, live reflectors, or special effects processors. Don't get me wrong; a recording space with good acoustics is great to have, but most of us with home or project studios are not designing dream studios. We're trying to do tracking in bedrooms, basements, and general living spaces. Most rooms are too small and too square, and share other functions. We need to work with what we have and make our "available" space do double duty.

All forms of baffles fall into one of two categories: enlivening or deadening. Live baffles enhance reflections—like the inside of a shower. Dead baffles absorb sound—like the inside of a clothes closet. In fact, I use my clothes closet. It comes pre-furnished with lots of soft sound absorbers: clothes. Sometimes I add a couch pillow to the back wall and/or the inside of the door. It's particularly effective with guitar and bass amplifiers. You can place the speaker cabinet (the whole amp if it's a combo) in the closet with the microphone(s).

For a livelier sound, remove the clothes from your closet or use a bathtub/shower surrounded by fiberglass or, better yet, hard tile—the sound will be extremely live. By adding or subtracting absorbers, you can dramatically change the liveliness of a space. If your spouse frowns on you laying furniture cushions against the floor and walls in assorted closets and rooms, you can build inexpensive baffles and keep your marriage, too.

Wall Baffles

Wall baffles, known in studio parlance as *gobos*, are small walls or barriers of sound-absorbing material that can be used in front of hard surfaces, in corners, or even between musicians to provide some sound isolation. To make one, build a small wall frame of the appropriate size with 2"x4" or 2"x6" lumber. You can make the back of the frame stronger by attaching a sheet of 1/4" plywood. You can also use Styrofoam or corkboard, both of which absorb some sound and are lightweight, but I dislike some of the crumbling that occurs with both materials and find that the 1/4" plywood also provides bracing.

For baffle filler, you have several options. You can stuff the baffles with heavy blankets or pillows, but my favorite filler is polyurethane packing foam. You'll occasionally get equipment packed in foam-lined boxes—keep the foam for baffles. While you're probably familiar with foam in slabs, it also comes flat on one side and undulating on the other; this is very effective in absorbing sound at most frequencies. Although you can use a piece of foam that fills the full cavity, you don't have to do it that way. Two layers of thinner foam with a space between them is also very effective. The dead air space between them creates a sonic trap that improves dampening. The greater the space and the thicker the wall, the better the effect. If you want a more finished baffle, you can cover it with fabric.

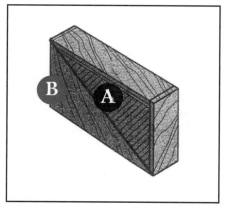

Wall Baffle

 Foam or other fill

B 1/4" plywood back

Because one side of this baffle design is absorptive and the other (the plywood) is reflective, you can liven up a dead space by turning the baffle around and using the plywood as the front. If you add a sheet of plastic laminate (e.g., Formica), the reflections will be stronger and reflect higher frequencies. The harder the surface, the more efficient the reflector.

If you want to build a gobo that will be used primarily for isolating musicians from each other, you need to make *both* sides absorptive, not just one side as described above. You can achieve this by placing the plywood in the center of the frame and absorptive baffle filler material on each side.

Amplifier Baffles

While closets work well for speaker cabinets, they can be a hassle for combo amps when you want to change settings. You can solve this problem by using what you've learned above to build an amplifier baffle, which will allow you to mic a loud amp while keeping the sound levels from overwhelming your studio.

Instead of building a small wall, construct a frame for a bottomless box that fits over your amp and completely encloses it. However, make sure to build it large enough for your amp *and* for the microphone and stand you intend to use.

Be very careful that you don't keep this box on the amp for an extended period of time. Heat can build up—especially from a tube amp—which can damage your amp or even cause a fire.

Amplifier baffles can be particularly convenient on amps with enclosed backs. For these, make a simpler and smaller open-sided box baffle, weatherstrip the edge, and place it up against the front of the amp to seal the sound inside. In this setup, the heat problem is minimized because the box doesn't surround the entire amplifier. You can even cover it with matching vinyl or Tolex.

Practically speaking, the box amplifier baffle works best with small recording amps. Their smaller size and great tone at lower volumes make the demands upon the box acceptable. This technique becomes unwieldy with a stack of Marshalls or bass amplifiers pushing out low frequencies with gobs of power. The bigger amps are better handled with closets and separate rooms. And if you have any old mattresses, they make great sound absorbers.

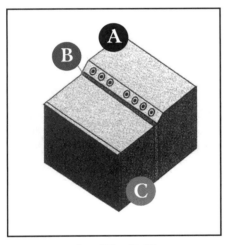

A Close-back amplifier

B Weather stripping

C Open-sided box baffle

Amplifier Baffle

Blanket Tents

Blanket tents are useful for big amplifiers, drum sets, and to separate playing musicians during tracking. If you go this way, be prepared to provide headphones to the musicians, and all that goes with them (i.e., headphone amplification and mixes).

Tents can be very involved. The supports are usually ropes tied to the walls. But don't tie ropes to your furniture unless you're looking for an excuse to replace it. Blankets get heavy quickly, and if you use carpeting, the tent gets heavier that much more quickly. Basements and garages make excellent locations for tent baffles.

You want a tent to provide isolation on five sides. You need to leave the front open to provide for ventilation for the musician who'll be playing in there. Five sides (top, bottom, left, right, and back) will do an adequate job. For the bottom, make sure that the floor is carpeted or has some other soft surface.

To build a tent, string a rope from the back wall of your room to the front wall on the left side, and then string another one parallel to the first rope on the right side. The distance between these ropes will be the width of the tent. Next, string a rope near the back wall and between the left and right ropes; this rope will hold the back blanket. Now, string several more ropes, moving toward the front, between the side ropes to support a ceiling blanket. Because the side ropes are supporting all of the weight, be sure that they are large enough to carry whatever load of blankets or carpets you plan to use, or the tent won't be up for very long. I suggest using heavy moving blankets because they offer a great deal of sound absorption, but are more flexible and lightweight than carpeting.

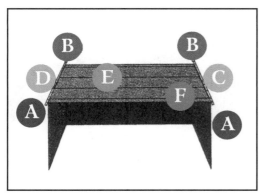

Blanket Tent

A Tie fronts of ropes to hooks in wall or other sturdy support able to hold weight of blanket

B Hooks in wall

C Right-side rope

D Left-side rope

E Ceiling ropes

F Top blanket

If you want the ultimate in tent isolation, use a double-walled tent to create a sonic trap between the walls. I once experimented with spaces up to 1' and was astounded by the deadening effect. The larger spaces (8"–12") better trap the lower frequencies.

The techniques described here are not high-tech, but they're effective and very inexpensive compared to adding isolation booths to your home. For most of us, the temporary use of a closet or room can provide ample control. But when they won't work and you want that certain sound that can come only from an amplifier when it is driven fairly hard, a baffle or tent will work well, keep the family at bay, and reduce your own listening fatigue.

The Basics

Adapt the above ideas to meet *your* needs. Just remember the following basics.

Soft Materials Absorb Sound

Think thick moving blankets, pillows, carpet, cork, curtains, cushions, quilts, bedspreads, clothes, mattresses, plush furniture, etc.

Hard Materials Reflect Sound

Think wood, glass, stone, cement, laminate, bathroom tile, fiberglass sheets, bricks, etc.

If the Material Insulates to Limit Heat Flow, It Generally Limits Sound Equally Well

Think fiberglass insulation, Styrofoam sheets, urethane foam, etc.

Also, remember that while high frequencies are easily absorbed by shallow surfaces such as a towel or a thin blanket, lower frequencies require some depth in the absorbing material. In this case, you need pillows, clothes, and the sonic trap approach. Remember—try to provide spaces of 8"–12".

By carefully thinking about what you need to do, the available materials, and the limits of your own space, you can use the techniques most amenable to your situation and get excellent double-duty use out of the spaces you have at your disposal.

How to Construct a Sound Panel
By Levin Pfeufer

Tools You Will Need

1. Tape measure ("measure twice, cut once")
2. Saw (or have your wood precut)
3. Dust mask (a must for dealing with insulation)
4. Brad nail pusher (prevents bruised fingers and bent nails)
5. Hammer (lightweight)
6. Nail set (for countersinking nails)
7. Fabric scissors
8. Staple gun (for medium-length, flat staples)
9. Glue gun (use clear-drying glue sticks)

How to Put It All Together

Choose your location, determine the appropriate size for your sound panel(s), and calculate the materials you'll need. Cut your wood (or have your material supplier help you). Buy your sound insulation and choose your fabric cover. Velour is a good choice.

1. Use a French cleat to attach the sound panel to the wall. This type of cleat can be made with two 3/4" strips of plywood—one mounted on the wall and one on the panel. Have a 45-degree angle cut along the edge of the two pieces of the cleat so they can interlock once mounted.

2. Use a 1/4" sheet of Luan for the sound-panel backing, (1/4" Ply or 3/4" Ultra Light will also work).

3. Frame the panel with 2" solid wood molding. For a more professional look, use molding that's channeled.

4. Fill the panel with soundproof quality insulation. Use insulation that is the same thickness as the width of the molding.

5. Staple the fabric into the rebated channel. Work from the four center points, rotating clockwise out, until you reach the corners. Then repeat the stapling pattern counterclockwise. Once the fabric is in place, use a utility knife to remove the excess, cutting carefully around the edges. Run a bead of hot glue over the staples and edges of the fabric to seal it. Rub your finger over the glue to flatten it as it dries.

6. Use a brad nail pusher and nail set to fix the 1/4" round over the staples and into the molding's channel, if there is one.

7. Hang your panel on the wall. For ceiling mounting, use hook-and-eye hardware.

Stupid Mic Stand Tricks

By Emile Menasché

Trying to get a clean recording in many home studios can be about as easy as losing weight on a diet of Boston cream pies. Even if your gear is in pristine condition and your signal path is as pure as an audiophile's ear canal, you're likely to be working in an environment full of ambient noise, poor isolation, and other acoustical distractions. One of the advantages of pro facilities is that, in addition to having floating floors, soundproof rooms, iso-booths, and acoustical treatment, they also have professional quality mic stands and shock mounts, which prevent unwanted rumbles from making their way onto your tracks. Below are some low-cost tricks you can use to help isolate your tracks using common mic stands and materials easily found around the house or at the hardware store.

Stabilize That Mic Stand

Remember those plastic weights you bought to help you rebuild the Adonis body you had in college? Do you remember where you packed them away? Good, because now you can set up for your next session, work out, and justify the fact that you never like to throw anything out, all in one easy step. Inexpensive mic stands are notorious for having wobbly bases. If your mic stand has a round base, unscrew the base from the pole. Slip one of the weights onto the bar, and put the base back in place. Your stand will now be much less likely to tip over. Ten- to 25-pound weights work best. If you don't have any, check out some garage sales—the sellers will be very grateful.

Float Like a Butterfly

Another common problem is noise that is transmitted from the floor to the mic stand and then onto the mic itself. This is an especially thorny problem if you're dealing with drums, loud guitar amps, or other sources that literally shake the house.

Rubber and neoprene doormats make excellent isolation tools. Cut the doormat into small strips and lay the strips under the base of your mic stand. The material will absorb much of the vibration of the floor. You can further enhance the absorption by using small squares of old carpeting in addition to the rubber. When dealing with an amplifier, place the amp on a chair or other stand, and use the rubber/carpet combination to isolate the amp from the chair, the chair from the floor, and the mic stand from the floor. You should notice a substantial difference.

Blanket Protection

You can help tame the acoustics of a reverberant room and even provide some degree of isolation using a boom-type mic stand and some blankets. Set up the boom in the shape of a "T," with the main stand telescoped as high as it will go. Drape blankets over the "T" (the stand shouldn't tip over if you've applied the trick with the weights). You can use these blankets to help curb sound waves from reflecting off the walls and ceiling and adding an unwanted room character to your track. One application that works well: Set up the blankets as a backdrop behind a vocalist. The mic will face the blankets, so reflections off the back wall won't get to the mic.

Goin' by the Book

Miking drums can be a chore, especially if you want to isolate individual components of a drum kit, such as the snare and hi-hat. You can create a mini isolation panel with a gooseneck mic stand, a universal mic clip (available just about anywhere), and a thin panel of a hard substance (a children's book is almost ideal). Clip the panel to the gooseneck stand and position it between the capsule of the snare drum's mic and the hi-hat (or vice versa). This technique won't entirely eliminate bleed, but it will reduce its severity as well as the frequency content of the offending sound. This should make it easier to further isolate each individual track with noise gates and to shape each track with EQ.

Function over Beauty
A Do-It-Yourself Keyboard Stand
By Jon Chappell

Here's a quick do-it-yourself project that will ease you into the world of carpentry and give you a valuable piece of furniture—a keyboard stand.

A keyboard stand supports either the piano-style instrument for MIDI and audio or the alphanumeric variety used to input computer data. Ideally, you should be using a keyboard stand for either of these tasks and not a tabletop. A tabletop is too high for keyboard work. Sitting in a standard desk chair and hoisting your hands over a normal 30"-high desk to operate a keyboard creates an incorrect and uncomfortable angle for your hands. Prolonged work at this angle can lead to cramping at best, and repetitive stress injuries at worst. That's why typists had those old-style short typing tables on wheels and why some office furniture features an under-the-top pullout drawer for the computer keyboard.

So here's a good stand that you can make in less than an hour, and for about $10—less if you scrounge. You can probably borrow the tools you need if you don't already have them.

The Project

When you approach any construction project the first thing you do is . . . start cutting wood? No, you write down your plans. Even if your visual arts abilities are meager at best, you need to draw your plans for two reasons: It makes you visualize the dimensions of your project, and it enables you to assess your material needs. If you see that you need 13 2"x4" boards of various lengths, you can figure out on paper how many 8' lengths you need to buy (8' is the length in which they're sold), how many cuts you'll need to make in the wood, and what tools will be needed to create your project.

In this project, you can use nails or screws interchangeably. If you just want to slap this puppy together, use nails, because it won't make a bit of difference to the ergonomics. Just don't be surprised when after a while your project starts to look like furniture out of a Picasso painting.

Take a look at the drawing to see how the various pieces fit together and about how much labor is involved. If you decide to paint the wood, do that before assembly. For functional furniture like this, go with a black, brown, or white in a flat or semigloss finish. Good luck!

Materials List

Wood: One piece of 1" plywood, board, or whathaveyou, cut to 12"x36" (this is the top)
Four 2"x2"s, cut to 21" (these are the legs)
Two 2"x2"s, cut to 12" (these are the runners)

Hardware: Four 1-1/2"x5/8" corner braces
Eight #6, 1-1/2" flathead wood screws (make pilot holes in the top board with a 5/64" drill bit) *or* eight 6d 2" framing nails

Tools: Drill with 5/64" bit *or* a hammer
Handsaw or circular saw
Tape measure or straightedge ruler, yardstick, etc.

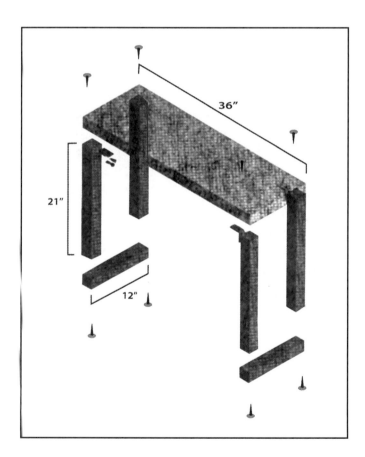

Cables and Connectors

The Quest for Signal Integrity
All About Connections, Cables, and Those Pesky Adapters
By Pat Kirtley

When I was a fledgling electro-geek, it was always a challenge for me just to get one gizmo connected to another. My first experiences in electronics were with the DC circuits connecting light bulbs, motors, and switches. In DC wiring, all that matters is that the wire is capable of carrying enough current and that the connections are solid. I then discovered audio and learned that transferring a signal cleanly from point A to point B is not as easy as sending some battery volts to a light bulb. When I tried hooking up a microphone to an amplifier using lamp cord and heard nothing but a loud, throbbing hum, I was perplexed. Like it or not, I had discovered the concept of signal integrity.

The term *signal integrity* refers to how clean and intact the audio signal is as it travels from one device to the next through the signal chain. At each connection and with each length of cable, the signal stands a chance of being degraded—by noise, interference, improper level matching, incorrect cable types, or flaky connectors. The purpose of this article is to help you hook things up correctly, and avoid some of the most common goofs in wiring your studio.

Connections

An audio facility or recording setup typically contains a collection of devices from different manufacturers, operating at different signal levels and voltage and interconnected in various ways. The *signal chain* is the path the audio signal travels through all of these devices and connections. The integrity of each path must be maintained for high-quality, clean recording.

At each junction between signal-creating and signal-processing equipment, the signal flows through cables and connectors of various types. Each connector type—whether it is a 1/4" phone plug, an XLR connector, an RCA "phone" plug, or a USB or fiber-optic connector—was designed for a specific purpose, and the most common audio connectors were designed many years ago. As a result, some connectors are better than others, and some connector types are more suited to particular applications.

Maintaining the best possible signal involves a series of trade-offs—for example, quickness and ease of use versus connection integrity. At one end of the scale is the XLR connector, typically used for microphones and mixer inputs; it is a robust connector, strong in both a physical and an electrical sense, and developed specifically for microphone use. You can leave these plugs in place for years without a problem, but the locking design isn't quick to work with if you have to plug and unplug cables repeatedly. These are also fairly expensive as connectors go.

At the other end of the scale is the ubiquitous 1/4" phone plug used in the early days of radio for connecting everything from speakers and headsets to non-audio devices such as switches and control units. Quarter-inch jacks are found in some form on nearly every piece of semi-pro audio equipment created in the last 50 years. They are easy to use and inexpensive, but are unreliable as "permanent" connections.

In the middle of the connector family is the venerable RCA jack/plug combo, first used around 1950 for connecting a phono turntable to its amplifier. The RCA was originally designed as a semipermanent connector—in other words, you can plug it in and leave it forever. It is now commonly used on both consumer and pro audio equipment, but the RCA plug has its pluses and minuses. The pluses are that it stays in place, provides a decent long-term connection, and is cheap to manufacture. The minuses are that this connector type can be frustrating and unreliable if you have to plug and unplug it often, and the associated cables can develop annoying shorts and separations at the internal point of attachment.

The above three connectors, despite their potential problems, are the "good" ones—they do the job day in and day out in almost every audio application. Other connectors—those we love to hate—are responsible for recurrent unreliable audio performance. The number-one offender is the 1/8" mini plug found on nearly every miniaturized audio unit, from pocket DATs and minidisc machines to computer audio boards. This little beast wins the prize for being bad for both long- and short-term usage. It was originally designed in the early 1960s as a cheap and dirty headphone connector for use with pocket transistor radios. The standard was widely adopted for general use to connect microphones, line-level ins and outs, and even digital signal streams in miniaturized equipment. If the plugs and jacks are manufactured from the best materials and engineered to the highest tolerance standards, they can work reasonably well. However, in reality, you may have a high-quality gold-plated jack into which you insert a five-cent plastic plug attached to a device. When dealing with mini plugs and jacks, seek out the absolute best quality cables and connectors you can find; also note that this is a case where a tight fit is a good fit.

Level Matching

Audio devices operate at different levels. It is important to know the level of the sending device and to make sure that it matches what the receiving device wants to receive. Some input channels can handle a wide range of levels. Many mixer preamp stages can accept—with proper adjustment of the trim control—anything from a tiny microphone signal to the healthy output of a line-level effects processor. But many input stages work only with specific signal levels. For example, you usually can't plug a guitar directly into a line-level effects unit; its low-level signal isn't strong enough to properly drive the input.

There are three general audio signal levels—*mic level, line level,* and *speaker level.* Mic level is the weakest, most vulnerable signal, and the most sensitive amplifier stages are microphone preamps. These stages require the most attention to proper cabling and connectors.

Line-level signals are routed between various processing units and mixers. Line level is considerably stronger than mic level, but still requires correct cabling and protection from interference. There are actually two standards for line level, and both types appear in nearly every recording facility. One is the *consumer* or *semi-pro* level of –10 dBV, which is referenced to voltage (1 volt = 0 dBV), and the other is the old *professional* standard of +4 dBm, which is referenced to power or wattage (1 milliwatt = 0 dBm). Other than having different reference levels, they are incompatible in that the output from a +4 unit will overload the input of a –10 input and, conversely, a –10 signal is too weak to properly drive an input expecting to see +4 levels. In many currently available devices, the +4 or –10 standard is switch-selectable, but it is important to make sure that everything is set correctly.

The last level is that of power output stages—the path between amplifiers and speakers. Speaker level is the strongest audio signal, and its cabling requirement is significantly different from mic- or line-level signals. Besides operating at a higher voltage level, speaker lines also transfer significant power, and require much larger diameter wire gauges than mic- or line-level cables.

Shielding

Two major things to keep in mind when dealing with levels are *shielding* and *power.* The weaker the signal level, the more shielding is required to ward off outside interference. At mic level, the signal is tiny, so proper shielding is essential, but power is miniscule at this level, so the thickness of the electrical conductors is irrelevant. At speaker level, power is much stronger, so conductor gauge or thickness becomes the dominating factor. Because the amount of power traveling through the speaker lines is thousands of times greater than any signals in the air that can cause interference, shielding is not required. Line-level signals are a couple of magnitudes stronger than mic signals, but they still transfer very little power. Their cabling requirements are therefore less stringent, but shielding is still necessary; in a typical studio there are numerous line-level connections, so the quality and types of connectors you use is important.

Signals that can interfere with audio circuits are always present in the electronic environment. They can travel through the air (such as interference from nearby radio transmitters or fluorescent and neon light fixtures), and they can travel through the electrical paths in power cords and equipment (such as power-line interference from motors and electric company transformers). Some electrical environments are "quieter" than others, but unless you are in the middle of a desert running on battery power, there is always some level of background noise attempting to leak into your audio signal paths.

You need to be aware of the strength of the desired audio signal versus the strength of external interference. Speaker lines are almost fully insensitive to external interference, while microphone lines are constantly in danger of picking up unwanted electromagnetic garbage.

Cabling

Preserving signal integrity means using proper cables and connectors. Let's look at cables first. Nowhere else in audio will you find a more confusing set of choices or such an abundance of outrageous manufacturers' claims than in cabling—but it's easy to simplify the cabling picture. When you think cable—whether mic, line, or speaker level—think, in order, *proper type, signal level,* and *length*.

The quality of materials and manufacturing is extremely important for cables, whether they are preassembled cable-and-connector units or custom jobs you fabricate from parts. We've already talked about connectors, so let's examine cables. In general, audio cable is made up of metallic conductors surrounded by a rubber or plastic sheath. Manufacturers of quality cable design their products for use in different environments. Mic cables, for instance, must be flexible, resistant to crushing and mechanical damage, and well shielded. Line-level cables, on the other hand, don't require much physical strength or flexibility, but they do require good quality connectors and strain-relief fittings where the cable attaches to the connector.

Cable capacitance is another factor affecting signal quality. While shielded cables reduce hum and interference, they also create *capacitance*, which causes a loss of high frequencies. The amount is determined by the internal construction of the cable and its length. All coaxial cable has a specification of capacitance per foot. Capacitance is also influenced by the impedance factor of the associated devices. A high-impedance circuit, such as the input to a guitar amplifier or processor, is affected much more seriously than a low-impedance microphone mixer input. The rules of thumb are to keep all cabling as short as possible and to spend the extra bucks for special low-capacitance cables when connecting high-impedance signal sources over a distance of more than a few feet.

What about the special ultra-performance cables offered by specialty manufacturers? Sometimes they are extremely expensive. Is the added cost worth it? Generally, these products offer high-quality materials and manufacturing, and quality is never a bad idea. But as far as the claims made for "improved" audio, they may be true but they are difficult to quantify. Just remember that the primary requirement of cables is to *preserve* signal quality, not *enhance* it.

Balanced and Unbalanced Lines

This topic can seem confusing, but the basics are not difficult to understand. Two crucial concepts are *grounding* and *shielding*. In general, grounding means providing a path through wiring back to an actual connection with the earth. For audio pathways, a true ground connection may or may not be required. Sometimes all that's necessary is a *signal ground*, which is a connection back to the metal chassis of a piece of audio gear. Shielding in audio is called *electrostatic shielding*. It can be thought of as a barrier through which unwanted signal interference—from commercial TV/radio, cell and cordless phones, industrial radios, large motors, and fluorescent light fixtures—cannot pass. Shielding is related to grounding because shields must be grounded to be effective.

Balanced audio lines have two signal paths, plus (+) and minus (–). The ground path (when used) is separate, so balanced, shielded cables have three connections. Most importantly, neither side of the signal path is at ground potential in a balanced line. In shielded balanced lines, the shield—typically a braided wire shroud around the two conductors—is connected to ground, or to the chassis of a piece of audio gear.

In shielded *unbalanced* lines, the ground is also the shield. The audio circuit, which always requires two conductors, shares the shield as its second conductor. Usually it works okay, especially if the audio signal is strong enough to exceed the currents from hum and interference. But when the signal is very weak—such as that from a microphone or musical instrument pickup—the balanced line always yields a superior passage.

Adapters

Adapters, although they can be necessary and helpful, are the bane of signal integrity. Adapters are devices that allow you to join connectors of different types. Whether it's in the world of plumbing, high-voltage power, or audio electronics, adapters are always problematic—however, we use them every day to make things workable. Be aware that adapter fittings, especially the general-purpose aftermarket variety, tend to be of lesser quality than other cables and connectors.

Since adapters exist to hook up virtually anything, you must be careful not to inadvertently use them in a way that compromises your audio. For example, you can't just use a wiring adapter to connect a balanced-line microphone cable to an unbalanced 1/4" input jack. Even if it seems to work, the signal integrity is affected. The way to make it work, in this particular case, is to use a transformer that converts the low-impedance balanced line to a high-impedance unbalanced input signal. It's not just a four-buck adapter you need here, but a high-precision audio component. Similarly, there are all kinds of "Y" adapters that allow you to send a signal simultaneously to two inputs. But is the sending unit capable of driving two inputs at once? Many can't, and this is another case where you need active circuitry to do it right, and not just a cheap adapter.

A good rule of thumb is to *use adapters only when they're absolutely necessary*. You should also be mindful of possible audio degradation because of their use. Don't leave adapters in place long-term in the studio—you'll *always* be happy you took the time to make or obtain the correct connections.

Digital Audio

The signal-handling options with digital audio are more straightforward than with analog connections and cabling. When audio is in digital form within a cable, it acts nothing like its analog counterpart. Cable capacitance problems don't chisel away the treble, and aircraft radios don't leak through and ruin a take. In many cases, two or more channels of audio travel through the same cable together.

But digital, as you might imagine, has its own set of rules and parameters that must be followed for a pristine signal chain. Digital audio signals are highly similar to the data that travels through an office network. In general, digital audio, when passed from unit to unit, either works or doesn't work, which is a good thing. But the lack of obvious cause and effect (such as the ability to wiggle a bad connection and hear static) can make troubleshooting digital signal chains difficult. Many of the same rules for analog still apply, however: Keep cable lengths as short as possible, and don't use adapters to hook up dissimilar connector types.

The Final Word

There are numerous places and ways to lose signal quality in any audio setup. It's important to use your ears to detect possible problems and to always keep the signal chain as simple and uncluttered as possible. Recording is an exciting adventure, and many issues vie for the engineer's attention. It's a lot more fun when you can eliminate annoying wiring and connection uncertainties and be confident that your sound quality is the best that it can be.

Ensuring Clean Audio in Your Studio

- Use the shortest cable lengths possible. With high-impedance unbalanced cables, degradation of high frequencies due to cable capacitance begins to show up at lengths greater than 10'. (Low-impedance balanced lines are less susceptible to this problem, and can be run up to 200' without problems.) With digital signals, the criteria are even more stringent: You should keep both hardwired and keep optical digital cable runs under 6" if possible. If you must exceed that distance, be on guard for data gaps and errors.

- Remember that different units operate at different levels. If the levels between units are too high, audible distortion may result. If the levels are too low, the added gain necessary on the input side will result in more noise. When it's possible to control both the output and input levels on the units in the signal chain, try to set the outputs as high as possible (without distortion), and set the input levels of the receiving unit accordingly for a clean signal.

- Many units such as effects processors do not have level indicators; it is possible to overdrive their inputs without even realizing it. One way to set levels by ear is to turn up the input of the unit (or the levels sent from an upstream unit) until you hear obvious distortion, and then back off the levels enough to ensure the signal won't distort, even with momentary peaks.

- If you experience a consistent hum or buzz in your studio, try to track it down with the following troubleshooting steps. First, determine if the hum shows up in several different pieces of equipment or multiple mixer inputs. If so, there may be a problem with the electrical system grounding for the building, or another wiring-related problem. Inexpensive solid-state lighting dimmers can also generate strong fields of interference. Second, track down hum problems that seem to be isolated to one piece of equipment. Inactive electronics and internal power supply defects can cause humming and buzzing; have the equipment checked by a technician. If the problem can be isolated to a microphone or other signal source, defective cables may be at fault.

- If you have cables that are constantly being plugged and unplugged, you can buy an inexpensive cable tester and routinely check them out. In this way, you can deal with problems away from the pressure of a gig. There are several easy-to-use testers available in a single multipurpose unit that can check all of the standard cable types.

- If you record on a hard-disk system, be aware that within these systems audio problems can show up as small, sometimes barely audible clicks and gaps in the recorded information. If you suspect these problems, try recording a constant tone from a signal generator at a fairly low level (say −10 dB below maximum), and then listen to the playback. If it is not absolutely clean, clear, and constant, you can look for problems within the computer. In many cases, these kinds of problems can be traced back to software issues.

- Always use high-quality cables and connectors from good manufacturers.

Cable Guy—Part 1
Wiring Your Own Cables Can Improve Your Sound and Save You Money
By Bill Philbrick

Planning a new studio can be such great fun. You strap on the old drool cup and imagine all of the wonderful toys—er, I mean *serious sonic tools*—you'll be using. Oh, the joy! Oh, the bliss! Oh, the nightmare when you suddenly remember that you must cable all of this stuff together!

Most inexperienced engineers use store-bought cables in their studios, but professional facilities almost always make their own or have them made to custom specs. There are several reasons for this. First, store-bought cable comes packaged in "popular" lengths, and these may not necessarily suit a particular setup. The mess that can ensue at the back of your rack (the professional term is *spaghetti*) can make it difficult to add new gear or track down problems; it can also be a source of noise. Cables with molded plugs are particularly bad because you can't repair them (without having to go out and buy new plugs). Forget death, forget taxes—the only real truth in life is that sooner or later, cables fail. And it often happens at, say, 2:00 a.m. when your mix *must* be delivered in a few short hours.

Another problem with inexpensive store-bought cables is that most of them are unbalanced. Unless you plan on limiting your studio to only a few pieces of unbalanced equipment—and plan to keep all of the pieces within a couple of feet of each other—unbalanced cables can mean higher noise and generally degraded sound.

Balanced vs. Unbalanced

Balanced cable is composed of two conductors and a shield. *Unbalanced* cable has one conductor, and the shield acts as the second conductor. Most pro audio equipment uses balanced inputs that employ *common mode rejection*. This circuitry passes signals of opposite polarity on two separate lines; the ground is on the third. The advantage is that any stray noise that may get through the shield will affect both conductors equally and thus be rejected at the input. An unbalanced line will pass the noise right through. This is especially critical with microphone lines, which carry very low signal levels followed by very high gain after the input stage. Whatever noise is present will be amplified by the mic preamp, right along with the audio.

Of course, if all of your gear has unbalanced inputs and outputs, this part of the discussion is academic. But this doesn't mean that you should go ahead and buy spaghetti. Whether you're running balanced, unbalanced, or, like most people, a combination of the two, you can improve audio performance and save money by building your own cables.

Bulk Up

You should use the highest quality (read: *most expensive*) cable that you can afford. There is a difference in the sound when using high- vs. low-quality cable, and it is not subtle. No matter what level of quality you decide you can afford, buying quality materials in bulk from a professional reseller and making your own cables can save you considerable money. Most of the professionals I work with favor Canare or Mogami brands. Beware of the cable you find for sale at consumer stores; the packaging may claim that it's audiophile quality, but it's really just astronomically overpriced.

If you're planning on wiring in a unit with multiple connections, such as an ADAT, try using *multi-pair* cable. A multi-pair is a large cable consisting of a number of groups of smaller cables. Since you need to break out the individual lines only at the connections, multi-pair is much neater and less bulky than simply tying together a bunch of individual cables. It's also a more cost-effective way to create multiple cable lines.

You can also save money and frustration by carefully measuring your studio and cutting all of the cable to length. If you're cabling a unit into a rack, be sure to calculate the amount of slack needed to comfortably slide the unit out of the rack from the front; 2' feet is usually plenty. This can save major headaches when you need to troubleshoot the unit. There's nothing more annoying than pulling a piece of gear out of a rack only to have the cables pop out and fall into the abyss behind the rack. Avoiding those extra miles of spaghetti saves money, prevents sound degradation, and is much less confusing when the need arises to go back there and trace something.

Compatibility

This is what customizing cables is about. There's a maddening lack of standardization among audio manufacturers. Some gear uses XLR with pin 2 hot. Others require XLR with pin 3 hot, or 1/4" TRS (Tip, Ring, Sleeve) with tip hot, or l/4" TRS with ring hot, or the ever-irritating 1/4" TRS tip send/ring return. And then there is ADAT gear, which uses Elco and D-sub connectors on some of its inputs and outputs. Prefabricated cables won't cover all of these contingencies, and even if you do eventually get everything hooked together, you're likely to spend the next six months trying to locate the sources of hum and buzz.

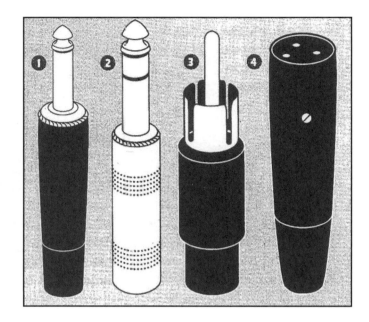

These are the four most common types of connectors found in home studios:

1) unbalanced 1/4" TS
2) balanced 1/4" TRS
3) unbalanced RCA or phono
4) balanced XLR or Canon

Always buy the best connectors you can afford. Switchcraft and Neutrik connectors are worth the added expense because they are durable, sound good, and are easy to work with.

Whether your studio is large or small, putting together an intelligent floor plan—with room for easy expansion—can help make your job of cabling easier.

In the next article, we'll take a detailed look at how to put the cables together and maintain them for optimum performance.

Cable Guy—Part 2
Tips and Techniques for Wiring Your Own Cables
By Bill Philbrick

The previous article covered numerous reasons why it is a good idea to make your own cables: It's cheaper, the cables are customized to length with proper connectors, everything is higher quality, and it's all easier to repair when necessary. For this article, the focus will be more on how to build your own.

Plan Ahead

When building a studio, a little planning prevents a lot of headaches. Before you begin, check the *gozintas/gozatas* (pronounced "goes-intos/goes-outas") of all of the different pieces of gear you intend to use, and remember: Studios grow. A year from now you will have more gear (often much to the chagrin of your spouse). Planning ahead by adding, for example, extra cables in the bundle that runs to an outboard rack, can make upgrading much easier and can keep things neat.

Plan where all of the different pieces of gear will go. Measure the length of cable required to get to each. Don't forget to allow extra slack so you can slide a piece of gear out of a rack without having to unplug it.

All cables should be numbered. Use adhesive numbers for cables, but then put a piece of clear shrink tubing over the sticker. This will prevent the sticker from moving or coming off, and will also keep the cable jacket from becoming gooey.

Referring to your list of gozintas/gozatas will tell you what connectors will be required. The list should include connectors needed as well as the *pin-out scheme* of the balanced cables—i.e., which points are hot, cold, and ground. The more common scheme is pin 2 hot, pin 3 cold, and pin 1 ground. In the case of 1/4" or bantam plugs, it's usually tip hot, ring cold, and sleeve ground. Beware: This is by no means universal. Many manufacturers make pin 3 hot. You *must* check.

Most home studios wind up using a variety of semi-professional and professional gear. This often means connecting balanced and unbalanced lines, sometimes from pieces running at different operating levels. In some instances, a matching transformer or other electronic balancing act will be required, but often one merely needs to tie pin 3 ("cold") to ground and possibly adjust the gain.

Tools and Environment

When you're ready to make your cables, you *must* set up a good workbench in a well-lit, well-ventilated area. A solid table is imperative. Using a wobbly, unstable bench is asking for trouble. You could be badly burned, or at least wind up creating more work and expense by damaging the parts you're working on.

You can order the tools you need from any good electronics supply house, such as Digi-Key or Mouser Electronics. I don't like to make enemies, but I feel compelled to say that every time I have resorted to buying tools or parts from basic consumer electronics chains that carry cables and parts (you know the places I mean), I have regretted it—the work has usually been accompanied by explosive amounts of frustration.

A good pencil-style soldering iron is the right tool for the job. The best irons have adjustable temperature settings, but these are not cheap. An iron of about 25 to 30 watts will do fine. It's wise to get a variety of tips for the iron, since you will work on connectors of several different sizes. Some irons come with simple stands, but many of these stands are fairly useless. Get a good coiled stand that keeps the iron off the table and has a space to hold a sponge. The sponge is important for keeping the tip of the iron clean.

Solder is available in many different diameters and tin/lead percentage compositions. I prefer to use good silver solder (which is actually tin/lead/silver) for a number of reasons, not the least of which is that it provides considerably better conductivity. There are also a variety of cores, with the most common being rosin. If you buy solid-core solder, you will need flux in order to get the solder to flow properly.

A good vise is a very useful component of your workbench (I'd like to have several, but my wife tells me that I already have too many vices). Again, many styles are available. My favorite has the abilities to open wide to accept many different-size parts and to actually clamp to the table.

Other items that should be living at your workbench include clippers, wire strippers, single-edge razor blades, small- and medium-sized needle-nose pliers, a pointed instrument such as an awl (used for many things, not the least of which is detangling braided shields), various sizes of flat- and Phillips-head screwdrivers, an assortment of shrink tubing, and a heat gun.

An optional tool that many people find invaluable is sometimes referred to as a *third hand*, which is like a set of stand-mounted alligator clips. It can hold a cable in place while your two hands are busy with solder and iron.

Go with the Flow

The essence of good soldering is flow. Enough heat must be applied for the solder to flow properly onto the part being soldered. Note that the heat is not applied directly to the solder, but to the part being soldered. Then when the solder comes in contact with the heated part, the solder will melt and flow onto the part. It's also a good idea to apply small amounts of solder to the parts that are to be joined; this process is called *tinning*. In our application—attaching connectors to cable ends—the wire is tinned and the contact on the connector is tinned; the two are then soldered together. The final joint should look shiny and clean. If it looks dull, then either the solder was not hot enough or the parts were moved before the solder cooled. This *cold solder joint* must be fixed or it will inevitably cause problems.

The sponge mentioned earlier is one of the most important parts of the equation. It should be kept damp, and the iron should be wiped frequently. A clean iron is imperative. Remnants on the tip of a hot iron burn and oxidize and, if not cleaned off, will get into the solder joints and fester. Occasionally, the iron should be tinned by melting some solder on the tip and then wiping it off so that the tip looks shiny and clean.

When soldering, "shiny and clean" should be your mantra.

The Convenience Connection
Simplifying Your Life (or at Least Your Studio) with Patchbays
By David Darlington

Did you choose a career in music only to find yourself spending most of your time plugging and unplugging wires? Do you spend more time underneath the mixer than in front of it? Does the back of your equipment rack look a lot like last night's pasta dinner? If you answered "yes" to any of these questions, your studio may be a prime candidate for a *patchbay*. A patchbay is a simple piece of hardware that provides centralized connection points for all of the gear in your studio so that you can connect the various pieces any way you'd like with short cables called *patch cords*. Instead of plugging wires into the rear of the equipment, you simply access each unit at the patchbay, eliminating the need for plugging and unplugging gear set up all over the control room. Patchbays come in various sizes and configurations and can be applied to digital gear as well as analog.

Point of Entry

Before installing a patchbay, design a specific layout for your studio, and keep accurate documentation of this setup. Determine how many *points* you will need to access. Points include all of the inputs and outputs of your mixer, the outputs of your synths, and the inputs and outputs of outboard gear such as mic preamps, compressors, and signal processors. Add up the number of all of these points and throw in a good number of "spares" for future expansion. You should also allow for a few extra groups of three or four for *mults*, which I'll cover a little bit later on.

Patchbays are rack-mounted units, which means that they are limited to a width of 19". The size of the connectors in the bay determines the number of points that fit in one row. The most widely used connectors are the familiar 1/4" balanced plugs, also called TRS (tip-ring-sleeve). Most 1/4" patchbays fit 24 points per row with two rows in a single rackspace for a total of 48 points per bay. Many professional studios use the smaller "bantam" or TT (tiny telephone) jacks that fit 48 across for a total of 96 per bay. Quarter-inch bays and patch cables are generally less expensive and usually can be easily installed, while bantam bays cost more and must be wired by a professional installer.

The back of a 1/4" bay has corresponding 1/4" jacks to accept cables coming from the gear, thus extending the gear's connection directly to the front of the bay. Once you have determined how many points you will need, you can decide what type of bay(s) would be best for your studio and how many you will need.

Logical Layout

The rule of thumb for patchbay layout is "out over in." This means that the output of a piece of gear shows up on the patchbay directly over its input. Following this rule, line-level sources such as synth outputs, guitar processors, or the outputs from outboard mic pre's should be directly over the line inputs; auxiliary sends from the mixer should be over the inputs of the various signal processors; and the outputs of the processors should be above the return inputs of the mixer. If you use several mic inputs at once, the output of the mic lines should be directly over the inputs to the mic pre-amps of the mixer (this requires converting the three-conductor XLR connectors to TRS connectors at the rear of the patchbay).

This brings us to a very important concept called *normaling*. Since patchbays generally occur in double rows, it is very easy to make connections between two points that fall in the same line vertically so that the signal will pass through even without a patch cord joining these points. This connection is called *normaled*, and a well-conceived layout uses these normaled points to keep patching to a minimum.

Here's an example. Let's say your mixer has two aux sends that you usually have plugged directly into your favorite reverbs, and the reverbs are returned to the mixer's stereo aux return inputs. If you were to bring these points out to your patchbay, you would have to use patch cords to connect them every time you wanted to use them. However, if the sends are normaled down to the reverb inputs and the outputs are normaled to the stereo return inputs, they will be directly connected at all times without any patch cables.

Synths can be normaled to line inputs, two-track outputs can be normaled to DAT decks or CD burners, and sends and returns can be normaled to signal processors. Using a patchbay means that all of these devices can be rerouted with patch cords into any configuration you wish.

Leaving Normal

Generally, when a patch cord is inserted into a point to reroute a device, the cord breaks the normaled connection below it. For example, if you want to patch your aux send to a piece of outboard gear other than the reverb, you usually won't want that send still feeding the reverb. In other words, you want the normaled point to be broken. Sometimes, however, there are certain connections that you may wish to maintain, even though the devices are also patched elsewhere. For example, your mixer's main outputs are normaled to your CD burner, but you want to record your mix back into your digital audio workstation for editing. If you patch the mixer to the workstation input, you still want to keep the connection from the board to the CD burner intact. This type of connection is called *half-normaled*.

Patch points can be normaled, half-normaled, or *non-normaled* (no connection between the top and bottom), usually by flipping a switch or inverting a module within the bay. Bantam bays must be soldered internally, so you must plan your layout before installation. Another type of internal connection is called a *mult* or *parallel*, and is just three or four points all connected to each other. This type of connection is useful for taking a single source to more than one destination. One possibility is to feed a stereo reverb with a mono send. Simply plug the mono source into the first point of the mult, and then patch the next two points out to the reverb inputs. If you have two mults, you can mult the left and right sides of your mix out to a variety of two-track recorders.

When you're first setting up a bay, planning and documentation are essential. Draw a frontal plan of your patchbay and carefully label each point for future reference. Use numbers horizontally to name the spaces, and letters vertically to name the rows. Point A1 is the left-most point on the first row, B1 is the left-most point on the second row, and so on. Keep a record of what gear is patched to each point. A good layout keeps common elements together, and the connections flow logically right to left and top to bottom. If you plan your layout correctly, after all of the gear is connected to the rear of the bay, your studio should function just as it did *without using any patch cords*. This means that you have optimized the patchbay layout with normaling.

Digital Connections

Just as analog gear can be rerouted with patch cables, so can all of the digital gear in your studio. Digital patchbays need to transmit audio signal as well as word clock through the same connection. Digital patchbays can be created using hardware connectors like bantam plugs, but more commonly XLR connectors are used for AES digital inputs while RCA connectors are used for S/PDIF inputs. Digital patchbays are often custom-made because they require so many different kinds of connectors.

Since AES and S/PDIF devices can only recognize their respective formats, problems can arise when connecting devices. The solution to this is an electronic digital patching matrix such as the Z-Sys Digital Detangler. In this type of electronic patchbay, each digital device is connected to the bay via its own format: AES, S/PDIF, or optical. The desired patches are then created internally through an electronic matrix that takes care of the format conversion and word-clock routing. Each device is represented on the front panel, showing which other device is routed to its input. With this type of matrix patching, one digital source can feed all of the destinations at once.

A patchbay can definitely increase your studio's flexibility. It may encourage you to use gear that would otherwise sit idle because it's too much trouble to plug in. It might also allow you to try new routing for your effects and signal processors. One thing it is sure to do is keep you away from the dust bunnies behind your gear.

How Patchbays Work—Signal Flow Summary

Patchbays create a central location where the inputs and outputs of your equipment can be easily accessed. Professional studios and location sound companies rely on patchbays to move sound between consoles, instruments, effects, and recorders. It saves time and creative energy, and reduces wear and tear on equipment. Here are a few examples of how the signal flow works in a patchbay.

Mixer to Recorder

Mixer outputs connect to the top back row of the patchbay. The signal flows to the recorder's inputs through the bottom rear row of the patchbay.

Multed Signal

Connecting the inputs of a second device (recorder, mixer, etc.) to the top front row on the patchbay causes the signal to be split or multed. The signal flows to the top front and bottom rear jacks simultaneously.

Adding Effects

Effects inputs connect to the top front row of the patchbay, and the effects outputs connect to the bottom front row. This breaks the signal from the top rear row to the bottom rear row on the patchbay, and the affected signal is passed through the bottom rear row and into the recorder.

Denormaled Mode

When a vertical pair of patch points is independent of each other and the signal does not flow down from top to bottom, the pair is in denormaled mode. The signal passes straight through the patchbay. You can denormal any channel by rotating the PC card 180 degrees on the horizontal axis.

Gear—Selection and Issues

More Gear
You Can't Live with It . . .
By Rusty Cutchin

When you work at a big commercial recording studio, there are several ways to have fun (besides the work itself). For example, you can tell your friends that you know how to align and synch up two 24-track analog machines, and what it actually means to "flip your inputs." It's also fun working on tons of expensive gear that someone else has paid for.

But in a home studio, you need to emulate all of that beefy equipment on a taco budget. There's a lot of duplication in a big studio—redundant capabilities that a typical home studio owner would never use, and gear only a finicky superstar producer would ever be interested in. A big commercial recording studio is full of stuff you'll never need . . . or will you?

Gear You Absolutely Don't Need in Your Home Studio

1 *Patchbays*

Who needs 'em? You're an artist, not a switchboard operator! Besides, your mixer has its inputs right on top where you can easily plug things in. And if you have to get to those pesky extra outputs on the back of a sound module, well, you're still young and wiry. You can get back there.

2 *More Than One Good Microphone*

What for? You saved up for that nice condenser mic—the one that sounds good when you and your band cop Chili Peppers tunes for your self-produced CD. It even sounds good on those nice flute solos your neighbor comes over to play.

3 *More Outboard Gear*

So a big studio has 27 reverbs. So what? Your digital multi-effects unit does everything: delay, compression, chorusing, pitch shift, bang, zoom. And if you need more than one of its effects, you can just print one to tape or disk.

4 **_A Bigger Mixer_**

No reason. You've got a nice 16-channel, four-bus board with good specs. It sounds great, and even through you have something plugged into every input, you can get by.

So you see, you really can stop worrying about all of that needless gear and start planning for . . .

1 **_Patchbays_**

Once you have 'em, you'll wonder how you got along without 'em. Think of your patchbay as a little audio file cabinet that stores every sound you might want to access. Having a patchbay means that even if all of your mixer inputs are taken up by drum machines, synths, mics, and hard-disk recorder returns, you can still get an extra sound source up quick, without unplugging something from the back of your mixer or equipment rack. It also means that you can get a full mix (with outboard effects) back into your recording system as soon as possible by patching directly into your recorder inputs, the inputs normally taken up by the group (bus) outputs of your mixer. Patchbays can enlighten and entertain you for countless hours.

2 **_More Than One Good Microphone_**

No matter how good your favorite mic sounds, it will never be the right mic for all purposes. And now that digital recording has leveled the playing field for home studio owners, the nuances of instruments and microphones can be heard clearly where they were masked before. Even the venerable Shure SM-57 and 58, beloved by working musicians, can make a remarkable difference when used intelligently and in tandem with a high-quality condenser.

3 **_More Outboard Gear_**

Get out your favorite mix (that is, one that you've worked on) and compare it to a commercial CD of an artist you really like. Chances are that you're still going to like the sound of the commercial CD better. There are many reasons why big records are made in big studios. One of them is that, in many cases, more really is more. Big studio consoles have compression, noise gates, and EQ on every track, and the studios have lots of external processors as well. Depending on the style of music you create, you can dramatically punch up your mixes by patching in access to different compressors and EQ modules. Of course, you might just want to consider buying . . .

Semi-pro digital mixers have become standard in the home recording world. Not only are they powerful, but they also include automation, more channels in a smaller space, and onboard dynamics processing—just like the big boys.

Even with all of this, remember: It ain't the tools, it's the carpenter. With ingenuity, imagination, and persistence, you can create some great-sounding recordings with a minimum of gear. However, if you're looking for "the big pro sound," you'll have to use some of that ingenuity to keep beefing up your studio.

Introduction to Microphones
All About the Essential Recording Tool
By Pat Kirtley

Blame it on Sir Charles Wheatstone. Way back in 1827 he was the first to coin the term *microphone*. You may not know that it would be more than 50 years later when the first device bearing the name was actually invented, but if you are a recordist, you'd better learn how they work. Microphone mastery is the most essential skill you need—right up there with knowing how to set levels and developing the people-engineering techniques needed to convince the band to finally go home at 3 a.m.

The first thing you need to know is that not all microphones are intended for recording. In fact, most are not. Every telephone contains a microphone; it isn't a very good one in recording terms, but it works fine for its intended purpose. Here, we'll concentrate on microphones designed for recording.

The Basics

In the simplest definition possible, a microphone is a device that translates acoustic waves into electrical currents. Doing this seemingly simple job with high quality and reliability is a task that has challenged engineers since the device's early days. Designers have come up with numerous styles and designs for microphones. The main types currently in use are *dynamic, condenser* (sometimes called *capacitor*), and *ribbon*. Ninety percent of all microphones are of the dynamic or condenser types. The quality of a microphone is determined by its frequency response, acoustic sensitivity, distortion factor, and internal noise factor.

No matter which method of operation is used, virtually every microphone has internal circuitry to condition the signal and send it to mixer channels and preamps in a uniform way. Every microphone also has a characteristic pickup pattern, which defines the way it responds to sounds coming in from varying angles over a range of frequencies. A good recording engineer needs to know much more about a microphone than simply how to plug it in and get a sound level. A true appreciation for the qualities of each microphone comes from studying and understanding its specifications, and then learning to hear its unique characteristics and exploit them in a real-life environment.

A Little History

The development of microphones parallels the rise of the recording, radio, and communications industries. The first practical mic was a carbon button microphone, and its invention in 1879 transformed Alexander Graham Bell's telephone from a laboratory curiosity into a device that literally changed the world. It worked by using a metal diaphragm to pick up sound vibrations and vary the pressure on a capsule filled with fine carbon granules, which varied the resistance to an energizing current in proportion to the sound pressure. For years, carbon microphones were used in telephony, broadcasting, and even in the first home recording setups.

Carbon microphones, though benefiting from an extremely simple design, had serious drawbacks for use in recording. Distortion was much too high, and frequency response was limited. They were fine for transmitting the spoken voice, but that was the extent of their usefulness. Music recording would require something much more sensitive and clean.

The earliest viable "high fidelity" microphone was a design called a ribbon mic. The basic idea was pioneered by RCA laboratory scientists in the 1930s and became a commercial product with the highly successful RCA model 77DX, which was used extensively in recording and film work through the late 1960s. By the 1950s, dynamic and condenser mic designs dominated the recording scene, and are still the pre-eminent designs.

Frequency Responses and Pickup Patterns

The starting point for evaluating any microphone is recognizing and understanding its *frequency response graph*. There's not much point in buying an expensive vocal microphone, no matter how good it looks, if its frequency response resembles that of a telephone. After frequency response, the chief characteristic of any microphone is its *pickup pattern*. Pickup patterns allow the recordist to select a microphone that will favor certain pickup directions and exclude others.

Frequency Response Graphs

To be able to relate the actual performance of microphones to their specifications sheets, it is necessary to be able to read and understand several types of charts and graphs. The most basic one is a graph of frequency response. Many electronic devices have frequency response graphs, all of which follow the same basic form. The lowest frequencies are on the left, and the highest are on the right. Usually, various frequencies are marked on the chart, and you can interpolate the others by the grid lines. The vertical axis of the graph represents levels with weaker ones on the bottom and stronger ones on top. A typical microphone frequency response graph is shown below. Usually, microphone frequency response graphs are "normalized" in the vertical axis, with 0 dB at the middle. The plus and minus deviations go above and below the zero point.

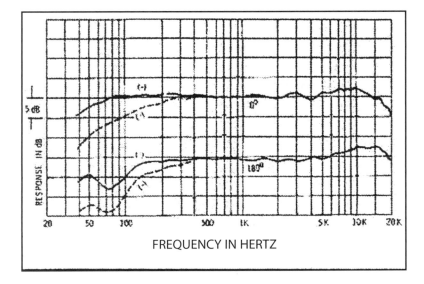

FREQUENCY IN HERTZ

The basic frequency plot is measured "on axis," with sound coming into the mic straight on in front. The first things to observe are the high and low frequency limits. These are the frequencies of the end points where the plot on the graph begins and ends, or the extreme points where the plot line begins to "droop" on each end. Typical response limits might be 40 Hz on the low end, and 15 kHz on the high end. Simple specs in the microphone manual would refer to this as "frequency range 40–15k." In general, the wider the span of frequency response, the better, but the frequency response limits by themselves do not indicate the quality of a microphone.

Next, look at the shape of the frequency response plot. The holy grail in audio electronics and reproduction devices is the ruler-straight *flat frequency response,* but typical microphone frequency response is not a straight line—there are usually a number of bumps and valleys. Some microphones have an overall "rising" characteristic, so that higher frequencies are emphasized. Many microphones feature an intentional bump across a particular range of frequencies. Depending upon the range chosen by the designers, this kind of boost can give a mic more presence on vocals, more crispness on acoustic instruments, or more heft in the bass ranges. Much of a mic's basic sonic character comes from its frequency response, which is usually determined by the objectives of the designers. In inexpensive microphones, the odd response aberrations you sometimes see are simply flukes resulting from a compromised physical design and might detract from the overall performance instead of enhancing it.

Pickup Pattern Graphs

To understand how pickup patterns work, you have to visualize the microphone "from the top." The graph that is used to show pickup patterns is a round graph called a *polar plot.* For microphones that are long tubes with the sound port at one end (i.e. a handheld vocal mic), you can imagine the tube being held horizontally with you looking down on it from the top. The direction along the axis of the tube is called zero, and the markings on the graph are set in degrees moving left and right from it, so that the direction looking straight into the side of the mic is 90 degrees (plus or minus), and the rear of the mic is at 180 degrees. For side-address microphones, the polar pattern is viewed directly over the top, with the mic standing vertically.

On this type of graph, relative levels are at a minimum in the very center and are highest at the outer circle. Once again, most polar plots "normalize" to a relative 0 dB at about the halfway point, and show plus and minus deviations relative to that circle. The

mic represented by the graph below is a cardioid (more about that in a moment). Maximum pickup is "on-axis" from the front or zero degrees, and minimum sensitivity is at 180 degrees, directly at the rear.

Every microphone has a pickup pattern (many mics feature adjustable patterns), usually one of four main types: *omnidirectional (omni), cardioid, hypercardioid,* and *bidirectional* (also called *figure-eight* pattern). There are other specialized mic patterns, known by names such as shotgun, parabolic, pressure-zone, and other increasingly exotic titles, but most mics used in studio work fall into the four basic types.

Mics with omnidirectional patterns are the simplest and least fussy of all to use. Ideally they pick up sounds equally from all directions. In reality, the omni pattern is far from perfect, with a definite fall-off in clarity for sounds from the rear, but when in doubt, omni mics are usually a safe choice. The cardioid pattern favors sound coming straight into the front of the mic and rejects sounds from the rear. Hypercardioid (and the similar *supercardioid*) is a cardioid pattern that rejects rear and side sounds to a greater degree, but shows its greatest rejection not at 180 degrees, but with dual insensitive areas at plus and minus 120 degrees from the front of the mic. The bidirectional mic pattern looks like a figure eight when graphed. It picks up equally well from the front and rear, but shows nearly total rejection of sound from the sides. This type of mic is very useful when used in advanced multiple mic setups in conjunction with other types.

Many microphones have been designed with multiple pickup patterns. This can be accomplished in a number of ways. One way—the simplest—is to have a mechanically operated port that can either open or close an acoustic chamber at the rear of the mic diaphragm. A better way is to design the mic to accept multiple, interchangeable, heads or capsules that are optimized for each pickup pattern. Classic studio mics like the AKG 450/460 series are typical of this flexible concept. When space allows, and price is of less concern, a designer can place two diaphragms in the microphone head, and through electrically combining their output in various ways, achieve a full range of switch-selectable patterns. This method is used in studio-standard mics including, for example, the Neumann U 87, the AKG C-414, and the Shure KSM44.

Patterns Aren't Perfect

To really understand the pickup pattern of a microphone, you must realize that the pattern's shape is highly dependent upon the frequency of sounds coming into the microphone. At mid frequencies, typically measured at 1000 Hz, the pickup pattern matches the basic shape of the polar plot. But at frequency extremes, everything changes. For omni, cardioid, and hypercardioid designs, the rear rejection is greater for higher frequencies, but at low frequencies—typically 200 Hz and below—all of these microphones become, in effect, omnidirectional! This is because low-frequency waves easily bend around an object the size of a mic capsule and aren't attenuated much. By the same token, high frequencies are easily blocked and diffused, so that they are lessened for sound sources approaching the mic from anywhere except straight on. These characteristics lead to some interesting behaviors in performance. In general, the "off-axis" sound of many microphones can be described as "duller" (i.e., containing less treble and more bass) than the on-axis sound. For some microphones, whose on-axis frequency response could be described as excellent, the off-axis tone can sound strange and hollow. The best mics have a very even sound over a reasonably wide angular "window." In general, omnidirectional mics are less affected by off-axis response aberrations than other designs.

Microphone Designs

Most of the microphones used in recording are of either the dynamic or condenser type. The only other technology of note (and still in use) is the ribbon mic. Many other technologies have come and gone over the years, but these two have shown staying power and are eminently useful in a number of applications. Both dynamics and condensers have survived and coexist because each type has strong and weak points for a particular usage.

Dynamic Mics—Universal Workhorses

The principal behind the dynamic mic is that of a loudspeaker in reverse. The same components are there: a magnet, a voice coil, and a vibrating surface (called a *diaphragm* in microphones). Instead of current from an amplifier flowing through the voice coil and causing it to vibrate within the magnetic field, external sound waves striking the diaphragm cause the coil to vibrate in the magnetic field and to generate tiny electric currents. Due to the simplicity of the design—and because designers can fabricate microphone components from a wide range of specialized materials—dynamic mics tend to be rugged, long lasting, and predictable.

The advancement in quality of dynamic mics has been primarily a process of refinement. If you could see inside the business end of a modern studio dynamic mic, you would witness a marvel of micro-engineering. Not only have designers found the best materials for diaphragms, coils, and magnets, but they have also discovered reliable ways to optimize the mic capsule for transient response, frequency range, sensitivity, and isolation from external mechanical noise. Dynamic mics are also intrinsically resistant to damage by high sound pressure levels—much more so than most condenser mics.

Where do dynamic mics show an advantage? Any time ruggedness and harsh conditions are concerns, the dynamic is the first troop into battle. Harsh considerations include the humid breath of a close-up screaming vocalist and the high sound pressure levels inside a kick drum. In terms of acoustic response, a dynamic mic's typically less extended high-frequency response can be a mellow alternative to the clinical accuracy of condensers for miking electric and acoustic guitars and basses.

The dynamic mic's simplicity is also an advantage. Its internal electronics are very basic (usually just a shielded transformer), and there is no need for a battery or an external power source. The mic is virtually a self-powered sound generator. There is less that can go wrong, and fewer settings to fiddle with. When you're doing remote on-site recording, these advantages become obvious. Some of the best live recordings you ever heard were made with a battery of road-weary Shure SM-57s and 58s. The "inaccurate," tone-shaping deviations of dynamic mics are highly useful. Instead of hunting around for an elusive EQ setting on the console to get, say, some punch in the midrange, you can swap mics and get what you need instantly.

When are dynamics not the best choice? If you require the precision of switchable multiple patterns, you should use condenser designs; dynamics come in only the basic flavors of omni, cardioid, and hypercardioid, and rarely do they feature multiple pattern switching. In audio terms, condensers rule when you want to capture delicate, quiet sound sources, such as voices, wind and string instruments, and percussion, or when recording big, full-range sources such as orchestras, string ensembles, or pianos.

Condenser Mics—Laboratory Accuracy

Condenser mics use the electrical principal of variable capacitance to translate acoustic waves into electrical currents. Overall, they are more complex than dynamic designs, and always have active electronic stages onboard requiring an internal or external power supply. However, in contrast to the high-tech finesse of the dynamic capsule, the condenser capsule itself is an example of simplicity. The diaphragm is a very thin metal or metalized mylar sheet, circular in shape, stretched across an insulating frame a very small distance away from a fixed, perforated, metal plate (called the *back plate*). A fairly high voltage called the *polarizing voltage* (usually around 100 volts) is induced across the two plates, and acoustic waves moving the diaphragm cause the capacitance between the diaphragm and back plate to vary. An associated electrical circuit translates the capacitance changes into voltage variations at the output.

The condenser capsule has a very high impedance—much higher than could be used by any preamp stage, and so high that the microphone's sound would be seriously degraded by even a short length of connecting cable. For this reason, a special amplifier circuit is built right into the microphone head to amplify the small signal and also to change the output impedance to a much lower value, which allows connection via cable to a preamp many feet away. The device that powers this initial stage within the mic is either a *field effect transistor* (FET) or a miniature vacuum tube. When you see the term *tube mic* it refers to the tube in this internal amplification stage. Tubes are a natural in this application because they have extremely high input impedance and strong voltage amplification characteristics. The drawbacks of tubes include the high current needed to power the glowing filament, and their need to be replaced as they wear out. FETs are great, too, with many of the same useful characteristics as tubes, but with the added bonus of much lower power requirements and a nearly infinite service life.

A variation on the classic condenser mic is the *electret condenser mic*. Mic designers in the late '60s discovered that the polarizing voltage applied to the capsule surfaces could be replaced by an electrostatic charge. The concept is similar to the electrostatic charge you get by rubbing an inflated balloon across a surface. The designers found that they could induce a more-or-less permanent electrostatic charge in certain polymer materials, and found a way to incorporate those materials into the diaphragm and back plate. The advantage of electret condenser mics is that they don't need the complex high-voltage polarizing power supply, so they can be made much smaller and less expensive. Almost all miniature *lavalier mics* (the kind TV news anchor people wear) are of the electret condenser variety. Electret mics need a power supply because they require the internal high-impedance amplifier/converter stage, however this power supply is much simpler—in many cases nothing more than a small lithium or alkaline internal battery. The better-quality electrets can accept either internal battery power or external power supplies (often referred to as *phantom power*).

Condenser microphones are a mainstay of studio recording. They are exquisitely sensitive to sounds over the full range of audible frequencies. If you are trying to capture a delicate, detailed sound, the condenser mic is your first choice. But by no means is it restricted to this type of sound source. Large diaphragm (1" diameter and above) condensers are the weapon of choice for recording vocals, although every singer's voice presents the engineer with a different set of problems, and most studios have a few large format condensers with which to experiment. Small format (3/4" and smaller diaphragm), tubular-shaped condenser mics like the AKG 450/460 series, Neumann KM84/184, and Shure SM81 (to name a few oft-used favorites) are mainstays in the studio for recording acoustic instruments and percussion.

When is the condenser mic not the first choice in recording? Usually it's a case of worrying about the financial investment factor. When you've paid a couple of thousand dollars for a microphone, you want to take good care of it. So while you'll happily put a pair of small capsule condensers up over a drum set to capture some airy ambience, you wouldn't consider letting your large-format side-address vocal mic go one-on-one with a cranked Marshall stack. Rugged dynamic mics readily tread where danger lurks, and precision condensers work just about everywhere else.

Ribbon Mics—Fragile Beauty

Not a common mic type, but one worth mentioning, is the ribbon mic. The principle on which they are based is quite different from dynamic and condenser designs. A wavy ribbon formed of very thin aluminum—or similar metal—is mounted vertically between the poles of a strong permanent magnet. Sound waves rushing past the ribbon element cause it to flex slightly, and since it moves within the strong flux field of the magnet, a current is generated across the ribbon. The internal guts of this microphone consist only of a magnet assembly, a ribbon, and a transformer to step up the voltage output.

Ribbon mics are unlike most other designs in that they have a figure-eight bidirectional pickup pattern as standard. That's because sound can enter the ribbon assembly equally well from both front and back. The figure-eight pattern in this type of mic is almost perfect; sounds from the sides are almost totally cancelled. Ribbon mics have a characteristically clean, crisp sound, and an intrinsically flat frequency response curve. They are excellent for recording large, distant sound sources such as orchestras and ensembles, and are equally good with close-up vocal work. Ribbon mics are relatively fragile though, and can be damaged very easily by rough handling.

Powering the Mic

Dynamic and ribbon mics are "self-powered," but condenser mics must have a power supply. The most common form of delivering the required voltage to the microphone is through a system called phantom power; DC voltage is delivered down the same wires that carry the microphone's output to the preamp or console. How can this be? There are three wires in a typical XTR mic cable: two for signal and one for ground. The DC phantom power (nominally 12 to 52 volts) is applied between the two signal lines and the ground line. In this way, no voltage is seen across the mic signal leads, and circuitry within the mic senses the voltage without interference from the audio. This is a standardized system, and just about any pro console or preamp can supply the correct voltage.

Electret condenser mics don't need a polarizing voltage on the capsule, but they do need power for the internal audio electronics. In many cases this is supplied by an internal battery, but the better electret mics can also accept phantom power if it is present. If you are running a mic from a battery, it should always be fresh, because noise and distortion greatly increase as the battery gets weaker.

Noise

All microphones generate a small amount of hiss noise, called *self noise*. Dynamic and ribbon mics show a very small amount of self noise, but condenser microphones, with internal active electronic stages, can have measurable amounts of it. In general, the better and more expensive the microphone, the less self noise there will be. Sometimes, a mic can have a fairly high self-noise factor, but this may not be noticeable if you are getting enough acoustic input to overcome it. Self noise is a problem when you are trying to capture weak, delicate sounds such as unamplified acoustic instruments. In these cases, better mics give cleaner results.

Another form of electronic noise is *hum*. Sixty Hz electrical waves are omnipresent in our environment, and sometimes we can hear this noise coming from microphones. The offending hum field can be introduced directly into the coil (for dynamic and ribbon mics) or internal transformer. Usually, you can correct it by moving the mic away from whatever is generating the hum field—generally, things like motors or power transformers in amplifiers. Sometimes, hum can result from a defective or damaged mic cable.

Filtering—Electronic and Acoustic

Modern microphones have wide frequency response, and sometimes it gets us into trouble. Both condenser and dynamic designs can have a frequency response that goes down to around 20 Hz, the lowest frequency most people can hear. In many cases, there are no sounds in this range we want to record, but the mic picks up environmental noise—from air-conditioning equipment, wind, nearby traffic, etc.—that we don't want to hear. In fact, we usually don't hear it, but its presence can quickly muddy up a recording. For this reason, microphone designers often include a switchable electronic *low-cut filter* in the microphone. Getting rid of random low-frequency energy at the mic is a good idea, although the action of these filters may sometimes seem too drastic.

The low-cut filter is also good for combating the *proximity effect*. This is a response characteristic found in cardioid and other *unidirectional* mics, but happily absent in omni and figure-eight patterns. It works like this: As the sound source gets closer to the microphone, the microphone's sensitivity to bass frequencies from the source increases, and the sound seems to get "tubby" or "boomy." Sometimes this proximity effect is useful (e.g., in making a male singer sound like he has more testosterone). But in other situations, such as recording an acoustic guitar, proximity effect is undesirable. The internal low-cut filter, usually centering at about 150 Hz, is great for correcting *proximity boom*. One of the cool fringe benefits of using omni mics is that you can get them up very close to a sound source with no boom and fully exploit the mic's low bass response.

Another kind of filter used with microphones is an *acoustic filter*, and it comes in various forms. Windscreens work by reducing the intensity of air blasts and wind movement. For vocal work, foam covers and nylon mesh screens serve well, but for recording outdoors in breezy conditions, those outrageously large muffs covered with feathers or light cloth are the way to go. In extreme conditions, the recordist can resort to a combination of physical and electronic filtering.

Though not a filter per se, an *attenuator pad* is included on many microphones. It is there to help to avoid overloads from extremely loud sound sources. Attenuator pads are found on console mic input sections, too, but the ones in microphones are better because they can tame overloads before they even reach a mic's internal electronics. Never switch in the pad if you don't need it, as doing so for normal sound level sources will seriously compromise a mic's overall performance.

Applications

Hopefully you now have some insight into how microphones work. Remember that when it comes to using microphones for creative recording, there are no rules. The key is constant experimentation tempered with common-sense technical knowledge. Happy recording!

A Glossary of Microphone Terms

Attenuator Pad: A switchable or removable internal electrical resistor that reduces the audio voltage from the mic capsule before it reaches the rest of the internal electronics. It is used when the acoustic level of target sound sources is very high, and it avoids overload distortion within the mic.

Balanced Output: A system of using two active conductors in a microphone cable for the audio signal, and a separate shield conductor that surrounds the two active leads. The balanced cabling concept avoids most external electrical interference problems.

Boundary Effect: When a microphone is near a wall or floor, or any large rigid surface, it will receive reflected sound from that surface at a fairly high level, but fractionally later than the original source sound. Depending on the distance, this can lead to apparent peaks and dips in the microphone's frequency response.

Cable Loss: Describes a phenomenon involving the loss of high frequencies due to the use of microphone cables that are too long (usually over 200 feet for studio mics).

Capsule: The inner subassembly of a mic diaphragm, coil, and magnet (for dynamic mics), or diaphragm and backing-plate assembly (for condenser mics). In general, the capsule is considered to be an integral unit, although it may contain many individual parts.

Cardioid: A directional pickup pattern that favors sounds coming in on-axis, and rejects sounds from the rear of the mic by about 20 decibels. The name comes from the root prefix "cardio," meaning "heart"; the cardioid mic has a characteristic heart-shaped polar response plot.

Condenser (or Capacitor): Describes a type of microphone that uses the electrical capacitance between a fixed plate and a moving diaphragm to generate audio currents.

Diaphragm: The thin vibrating part of the microphone that moves in response to sound waves.

Direct vs. Reflected Sound: Microphones "hear" sound directly from the source, but also receive sound that has bounced around the room and enters the mic from all angles. Directional mics tend to allow a higher proportion of direct sound by rejecting some of the bounced sound.

Directional: Describes any microphone that discriminates in terms of response for sounds coming from different angles. The greater or lesser degree of directionality is indicated by the microphone's polar response.

Dynamic: Describes a microphone that uses a diaphragm attached to a movable coil that generates a current via a permanent magnet structure.

Electret: A form of condenser mic capsule that permanently carries a static-electric polarizing charge between the back plate and diaphragm. The charge is retained by the use of special plastic-like materials used in constructing the capsule, and stays constant for years without recharging. Electrets do not need an external power supply for polarizing voltage, but still need a small DC voltage (usually from an internal battery) for the active audio electronics.

Figure-Eight: A polar response pattern that features equal response from directly in front of the mic, or directly behind, but rejects sound greatly from the sides. When the response pattern is graphed on a polar plot, it has the shape of the numeral "8."

Lavalier: A small mic that is clipped to a person's lapel or other clothing to pick up voice for television and radio work. Lavalier mics are also sometimes used in live situations to pick up the sounds of various acoustic instruments.

Off-Axis: Describes an angle other than on-axis.

Off-Axis Response: The frequency response of most microphones is somewhat uneven for sounds entering from any direction except straight on. Some microphones maintain very good frequency response at a fairly wide angle away from the on-axis direction. A microphone's off-axis performance can be visualized via its polar response graph.

Omni (or Omnidirectional): A pickup pattern that is nearly uniform for sounds entering the mic from any angle.

On-Axis: Looking straight into the center of the microphone's diaphragm. Also defined as zero degrees on the polar plot. Most microphones give their best performance with sounds entering on-axis.

Overload: When very loud sounds enter the microphone, the internal electronics can be overloaded, causing distortion that cannot be controlled by settings at the preamp or console. Overload can be controlled by using an internal attenuator pad.

Parabolic: A style of microphone that uses a parabolic reflector (it looks like a small satellite TV antenna dish) to focus the incoming sounds into a small microphone element.

Phantom Power: A powering system for condenser microphones where DC voltage is sent down the same wires that transmit the tiny audio currents to the console or preamp. Because the DC voltage is sent equally down both audio conductors (and forms a current flow only with the third "ground" conductor), it effectively cancels itself out at the console audio input. The advantage is that an extra conductor is not needed to transfer power to the mic's electronics.

Polar Response: A term used to describe the performance of a microphone over a full range of pickup angles. The polar response is expressed using a *polar plot*. There are usually several lines on the plot to indicate the varying polar response of the microphone over a range of test frequencies.

Pop Filter: A foam or mesh screen placed in front of the mic to manage "explosive" vocal sounds from vocalists. A pop filter is generally not needed when recording instruments.

Pressure Zone Microphone (PZM): A trademarked design of Crown International. A miniature microphone element is placed a precise distance from a backing plate, and picks up sound from the hemisphere in front of the plate. The advantages to PZM mics are greater working distance and even sound pickup over the hemispherical pattern.

Proximity Effect: The tendency of a microphone to accentuate bass frequencies as the sound source gets closer. All microphone patterns except omnis and figure-eights exhibit this effect. It can be counteracted by engaging a rolloff filter.

RFI: Radio frequency interference. Microphones and preamp stages, operating at very small audio voltages, sometimes pick up interference from nearby radio transmitting sources.

Ribbon Mic: A type of microphone that uses a thin, wavy aluminum ribbon which acts as a diaphragm/coil combination within a magnetic field to directly generate audio currents. The inherent pickup pattern is figure-eight, and the frequency response is extremely even.

Rolloff Filter: An internal electrical filter in the mic that can be switched in to lower the response at low frequencies. Some mics have a filter that allows the user to select from two different bass frequency points for more precise action. A rolloff filter is generally used to counteract the proximity effect.

Self Noise: The random background noise generated by the microphone itself, from its internal electronic circuitry (for condenser mics), or even from random electrons in the wiring (in the case of dynamic and ribbon mics). Some mics have low-noise electronics, and some have noise factors that are high enough to cause problems when picking up low-intensity sounds, so care is advised in choosing the mic for each application.

Shield: A metal covering or surrounding sheath that prevents external electrical fields from interfering with audio voltages in the microphone and cabling.

Shock Mount: A mounting system that holds a microphone within a cradle of flexible straps or bands. It is used to isolate the mic from low-frequency sounds coming from the building structure and transmitted through the microphone stand.

Shotgun: A highly directional mic, usually used in news gathering and film work, that can pick up sounds at a greater-than-normal working distance. It has a very narrow pickup angle and must be carefully "aimed" by the operator.

Sibilance: The non-linear response of a microphone to overenergetic vocal "s" and "t" sounds. Sibilance can be reduced by pointing the vocalist slightly away from the mic or by using external windscreens.

Side-Address: A microphone that is mounted in a vertical direction and accepts sound from the side of the housing instead of head-on like a handheld type. Most large-capacity studio microphones are side-address.

Supercardioid or Hypercardioid: Directional microphone patterns that favor sounds entering on-axis, and reject off-axis sounds to a greater degree than those employing the cardioid pattern.

Transient Response: The ability of a microphone to cleanly respond to very quick changes in the acoustic waveform, such as can be found in the sounds of drums and percussion instruments. In general, condenser mics outperform dynamics in terms of transient response.

Tube Microphone: A type of condenser microphone that uses a vacuum tube as the internal impedance translator element. Non-tube condenser microphones use a type of transistor called an FET (field effect transistor) as an impedance translator element.

Windscreen: A foam or mesh screen that goes around the outside of the microphone to minimize the effect of air movements that can generate unwanted low-frequency noises. Many microphones have small integral windscreens that are effective for moderate wind problems and for shielding the mic from *plosives* (e.g., vocalized "p" and "b" sounds). For outdoor location recording in moderately gusty conditions, a very large blimp-like apparatus covered with bird feathers is often used.

Working Distance: The distance from the mic to the sound source.

XLR: The standard three-pin connector system used on most microphones. The microphone has a male XLR connector; consoles and preamps have a female XLR jack.

What's So Hot About Tubes?
Why This Vintage Technology Is Still Champ in the Digital Arena
By Pat Kirtley

Warmth. Transparency. Depth. Fat, vintage sound.

We use these terms to describe the audio qualities of vacuum tube equipment. But what do they really mean? Well, tubes feel warm, thanks to a red-hot glowing filament inside. And most of them appear transparent, being made out of clear glass. But kidding aside, the flowery adjectives used by advertisers and copywriters are merely words, and words always fall short when describing sound qualities. But what are the real reasons why, in a world gone retro-crazy and suspicious of digital "sterility," vacuum tubes still have a place in our audio universe?

A Bit of History

For decades, the vacuum tube was the critical active element in audio radio, television, and all other realities of electronic communication. What began as a breakthrough idea for Dr. Lee DeForest in 1906 became the basis for the development of audio and recording as we know it. At the end of the 1940s, scientists working for Bell Laboratories invented the transistor and, soon after, the world of electronics switched over to solid-state designs in every area. Yet despite silicon dominance, tubes have made a comeback in audio electronics. Let's look at what makes a tube tick.

In the most basic type of vacuum tube—the *triode*—there are four basic parts. The first is the *heater*, which causes the cathode to emit electrons. The current flow of electrons is gathered by an outer element called the *plate*, and between the *cathode* and the plate is another element—an open wire screen called the *grid*. Small voltages applied to the grid directly control the flow of electrons from the cathode to the plate, and since the plate voltage is much higher than that of the grid, small signals at the grid are amplified.

Voltage vs. Current

To understand why tubes perform differently than solid-state devices (transistors and chips) you need to look at some fundamentals. One basic difference is that tubes are primarily voltage-based devices, and transistors are current-based. In a voltage-based design, you have high voltage and low current, and current-based designs are exactly vice versa—low voltage, high current. In fact, tubes are most advantageous in the areas of audio where small signals must be boosted by voltage amplification (e.g., mic pre-amps and line-level stages), while solid-state devices excel where power must be delivered to a load (e.g., amplifier output stages and power supplies). To handle a prodigious amount of current, such as that demanded by a speaker load, vacuum tubes must be made very large and rugged, while an equivalent output stage transistor is very compact.

In small signal stages, the relatively high operating voltages of tube stages—hundreds of volts, versus about 30 volts for transistor stages—allows for much larger undistorted output voltage swings. For transistors to cleanly produce large voltage swings, more transistors are used in complex configurations. A small signal transistor or chip stage designed for large voltage swings has many components. The equivalent tube circuit almost always has fewer parts and simpler design. Tubes are eminently suited for small signal amplification, and solid-state looks good for high-current power applications. Thus we find, for instance, hybrid guitar amplifier designs that have tube stages on the front end and beefy solid-state output drivers. It's a perfect example of the marriage of two technologies emphasizing the best qualities of both.

That's about all that is needed to explain basic tube functioning. Circuit design plays an important role too, as do manufacturing quality and the current condition of the tube. Like tires on an automobile, all tubes are destined to wear out, and long before they are completely gone, performance will begin to suffer. Tubes are trickier by far to maintain and operate than any other active electronic element, and have rightfully vanished from virtually every type of home and commercial device, yet they have popped up all over the place in contemporary audio gear.

What Is It About Tubes?

But is the vacuum tube a technology that we use because of its innate and irreplaceable audio qualities, or are we simply in love with the unique audio overload characteristics tubes exhibit? Resolving this issue can make the utilization of tube technology in our recording facilities more productive.

A lot is said about the "smooth overload" characteristic of tubes. The implication is that we want to overload the tubes. Is this true? Does it work? It certainly does. There are numerous guitar amps that are reissues of designs first conceived in the '50s and '60s. They sound faithfully like the originals, and the tones they get when deliberately over-driven are unique and wonderful.

But back to the topic of recording. Outside of using a real tube front end for preamping overdriven guitar sounds direct into the board, why do we care about how well something distorts? After all, the holy grail in recording has always been the absence of distortion. What about the clean sound of tubes?

I have never bought the idea that adding one or two measly little tubes into a recording chain will result in a glorious improvement—that passing the audio signal through a tube stage will impart some magical, mystical aura—but there are many current equipment marketers who would have you believe that it will. Their promotional writings hark back to a time when everything ran on tubes and analog audiotape—say, the early '60s. They cite the recorded quality of early Stones or Beatles albums as examples, and would have you believe that you will get a similar sound by buying their gizmotron with one pathetic 12AX7 glowing through the front panel.

They are trading on distant memories of bygone technologies. If you think about it, the only way to utilize that technology is to go to the vintage equipment dealers (or maybe the salvage yard) and purchase it. If tubes have a place in our current recording world, and we are not planning to spend our lives trying to revive electro-skeletons from the '50s and '60s, there must be something more. There is.

Tone Production or Tone Preservation?

There are two streams of thought, and two radically different reasons why people prefer tubes to solid-state amplification. In the realm of tone production, tubes are generally expected to produce distortion, and it is expected that it will be "nice" distortion that has a specific sonic character. Tubes and tube-driven stages in guitar amplifiers fill this role. The "clean" tone, with amplification stages well within their linear range, is not what tube sound is all about here. In tone production we are only concerned with the way tubes respond to being overdriven. The early war of tube guitar amps versus their solid-state challengers was completely about non-linear distortion characteristics. Tubes produce "even order" harmonics when overdriven, and solid-state devices produce "odd order" harmonics. Most everyone agrees that "even" harmonics are more pleasing, even musical—in other words, "good distortion." The sound of Eric Clapton's totally overdriven but eminently smooth and sweet tone from a Marshall stack at volume setting "11" is a good example of it.

The other direction tube lovers take is the appreciation of non-distortion tube qualities: the seeking of tone preservation. In this respect, we seek a characteristic of tubes that includes signal amplification—especially of signals containing significant peaks—without noticeable distortion. Does the introduction of a tube stage promote tone preservation? Some say "yes" and some say "no." And you can put away your fancy test gear when trying to get to the bottom of this issue because it won't be much help in finding the answer.

The difficulty of defining clean tube sonic characteristics can be illustrated by a phenomenon observed in television broadcasting called *film look*. Most people can see the difference between TV programs shot originally on photographic film and those shot on videotape. Most people agree that footage that originated on film really does look more pleasing and of a higher quality, yet no one has ever been able to define exactly what this difference is, or even why there is a difference. There is no meter or test device that you can use to measure or detect it, but the human eye can see it immediately. A further phenomenon is revealed when you notice that the higher-quality film originals still hold their quality difference when transmitted through the "lesser quality" video chain, including, at times, multiple generations of recording via videotape. It doesn't make much sense—if film-originated footage is superior to video, the quality should be lost as it squeezes through numerous video-processing stages. But this quality difference somehow remains.

Some observers would equate film with tubes and video footage with solid-state amplification stages. The analogy may not be far off. In the case of shooting with film, the light goes directly from the camera lens to the film surface, and the result is a whole different range of contrast and color characteristics than what you would find with light going from a lens to a video pickup tube. Some experts think that "film look" involves a subtle compressing of the contrast range that is more lifelike than what video cameras achieve. Everybody agrees that the look of film is better, with more depth and subjective appeal.

If the analogy fits, then the devices we audio recordists use at the earliest stages of the recording process—chain mics and preamps—are the essential place where vacuum tubes can make a difference. The recent proliferation of tube-based mics and preamps reinforces this notion. Most pro recordists agree that mic preamps are what define the character of recorded sound more than EQ compression or any combination of downstream devices.

Here's essentially why that is so. Raw signals from a microphone (and within the internal mic circuitry) contain more radical peaks than signals later in the recording chain. Researchers have found that huge—but brief—peaks occur often at preamp inputs. In other words, a preamp may have to routinely pass a signal that will drive its initial stages to distortion. It is agreed that tube stages sound more pleasing when overloaded in this way. Even though the overload isn't perceived as gross distortion, our ears detect a different tone color. This has been described as *clean tube sound*. As "film look" is regarded in the visual realm, clean tube sound contributes a unique quality to the recording chain.

Ultimately, the quality contributed by the differing technology is subjective and is an area where descriptive words fail us, logic fails us, and test equipment fails us. The character of the sound as perceived by the ears and brain is the final reading, and the ears tell us something as surely indescribable as the colors of a sunset, but as clear as the scribbling on a truck-stop bathroom wall. When we seek the preferred active devices in sound acquisition by high-quality mics and preamps, tubes rule.

Anatomy of a Tube Number Code

One example of the coding used to identify tube types is that used for the common tube 12AX7. But what does the alphanumeric name mean? The number of heater filament volts is "12," "AX" is a code indicating the specific design characteristic of this model, and the number "7" represents the number of internal elements.

To identify a power tube named 5L6GT, you should understand that "5" is the number of volts for the filament, "L" is for the specific design type, "6" is for the number of internal elements, and "GT stands for "glass tube." These codes represent the *American system,* and other countries such as England have their own naming systems. Most British designs begin with "E," as in EL34 or EF86; the prefix "KT" also indicates a British design. In many amplifier designs (especially hi-fi and guitar amplifiers), it is not unusual to find a mixture of U.S. and British tubes in the same piece of equipment.

Tube Quality Is a Downhill Slide

Unlike solid-state electronics—whose elements are so controllable at the manufacturing stage that units made up of transistors and chips are all virtually identical—tubes are much more variable. Things that affect tube performance are manufacturing factors such as degree and quality of vacuum, quality of metals, accuracy of element positioning, and amount of residual gasses left after the envelope is evacuated. Then, there are eternal factors that affect performance: ambient temperature, age, accuracy of heater voltage, and current flow in the circuit. If all of these factors are not carefully controlled, we end up with tubes that are noisy, weak, and *microphonic* (i.e., able to transmit physical sound like a microphone), and produce unwanted distortion.

We have grown accustomed to forgetting about the electronic inner workings of audio gear. Solid-state equipment just plain *works*, and usually works in a consistent way for years. But tube equipment must be monitored and babied or performance will suffer. For equipment in daily use, especially where power output tubes are used, yearly tube replacement is mandatory for top-notch performance.

A Glossary of Tube Terms

Dual-Element Design: Some tubes are actually two complete sets of elements (each collectively called a *section*) in one glass envelope. In the American tube-naming system, tube codes beginning with "12" are a giveaway for dual-section designs. Why? Most tube filaments are actually designed to be fed by six volts. In a dual-section tube, two six-volt filaments are wired in series, requiring 12 volts to light up the tube.

Envelope (noun): The glass outer casing of the tube. Envelopes are actually formed from tubular glass stock of which the ends are melted at very high temperatures to create a hermetically-sealed, evacuated interior. Sometimes you will find tubes with metal exteriors. The metal is just a protective outer covering over the glass to increase ruggedness and provide electrostatic shielding. Inside, it's glass—always.

Gassy Tube: The inside of a tube is supposed to be a nearly perfect vacuum, but perfect vacuums are rarely achieved. There are always some residual molecules of oxygen, nitrogen, and other atmospheric gases, as well as weird gasses that boil off of internal metal surfaces. If enough voltage is present, these gasses sometimes glow (especially in power output tubes) with an eerie blue aura. In general these gasses are undesirable, reducing the efficiency of the tube. In small-signal tubes, detrimental gasses can affect audio performance but don't show up visually.

JAN (Joint Army-Navy): On a really old tube envelope or box, you may find a JAN designation. It usually means that the item was manufactured for (and purchased by) the military. In other words, it's government surplus.

Matched Pair: Especially in power output stage, tubes are used in mirror-image pairs. Specially selected pairs are tested at the factory and, via a measurement process, found to have extremely similar characteristics. You buy these in sets of twos or fours, boxed together, and the premium price reflects the cost of the matching process.

Microphonics: Sometimes the metal elements inside a tube can move slightly and cause the tube to transmit physical vibration, like a microphone. This problem is most likely to be apparent in high-gain preamp stages, and is a most unwelcome situation. The only cure is to replace the offending tube with another, higher-quality unit.

MIL-SPEC (Military Specification): Tubes originally approved for use in military equipment have a special code number series. Generally, tube codes that are all numerals (e.g., 5227 or 5881) represent the MIL-SPEC equivalent of the standard tube-type codes.

NOS (New Old Stock): The demise of tube technology in the mainstream left warehouses literally full of tubes; many manufacturers shut down production lines forever. These tubes were new until they sat there in their boxes for years and got, well, "old." But they were still *like* new because they were never used, and many aficionados believe they are better quality than some being manufactured today. Like anything with a cachet of "antique-ness", they command a premium price. Some rare tube types are no longer manufactured at all, and are only available from the NOS suppliers.

Power Tubes: These are also called *beam power tubes,* and are found in output stages that drive speakers. They are physically much larger than small-signal tubes, consume much more operating current, and throw off prodigious amounts of heat. They also have shorter working lifespans due to higher heat and electrical stresses.

Premium Tubes: You can pay more money to get "premium" tubes that have been pre-tested and found to meet certain quality criteria—a process not too different from the grading of eggs for the supermarket. There are also tubes manufactured to a higher-than-normal standard, with things such as gold-plated pins and special metals; they, too, command higher prices.

Shield: Sometimes, in small-signal tube circuits, you may find a metal can placed over a tube. This is a shield to keep stray electrical fields from affecting the tube's quiet performance. If it is removed, it should be replaced. You also may encounter a *self-shielded* tube design with a fine wire screen cage inside the glass envelope.

Small-Signal Tubes: These are physically the smallest of the tube family, and are designed for voltage amplification. In the realm of recording, they are the workhorses, and fill a number of roles ranging from straight amplification to EQ to compressors.

Tube Substitution: Sometimes various tube numbers can be used interchangeably. Substitution involves using one type in place of another. Using an "equivalent" tube (i.e., a MIL-SPEC model in place of a generic code) is fine, and there are charts available that list direct equivalents. For instance, a British ECC82 can replace a type 12AU7. Substituting tubes without being sure of the equivalence is dangerous business, especially in power output sections where plugging in an incorrect type can cause the destruction of the equipment or the tube.

Warm-Up: Tubes require a period of time to reach a uniform operating temperature. Before that period of time has elapsed, the tube may exhibit noise, insufficient gain, and higher distortion. Some experts think that a minimum of a couple of hours' warm-up is necessary to achieve optimum performance.

Calibration
How to Make Sure Your Gear Is All on the Same Page
By Pat Kirtley

Your life as a recordist gets a lot easier when all of your recording and mixing equipment agrees with each other in terms of levels. Until the time comes when all of these machines are sporting fully digital interconnects, there will be a need for the process called *level setup* or *calibration*.

One type of calibration is done to ensure that a certain reading on a level meter will result in a certain amount of activity on the recording media. This type of calibration takes place within the inner circuitry of the device itself, and won't be covered here. But there is an important need for level agreement *among* devices, too. When this is properly accomplished, it does wonders to increase your level of confidence and working efficiency, and you can learn to do it yourself.

In full-blown pro studios, this work crosses into territory covered by a maintenance engineer—but you probably don't employ a maintenance engineer, so the following is a simplified method that is definitely non-tech but achieves good results. Traditionally, this process requires test equipment and someone who knows how to operate it, but let's look at a DIY approach that requires neither.

First, get your hands on a test-tone CD. There are various types of these available, from NAB, Denon, Sheffield, and others. Turn *off* your monitor speakers before proceeding—these test-tone levels could kill them! Using a CD player in good condition, play the "1000 Hz 0VU" test tone with the player connected to a line input on your mixer (or all-in-one MDM). Set the channel fader to its "0" marking (usually near the top of its travel; sometimes the midpoint on rotary level controls). Now, while watching the mixer's main output meters, raise the master fader until the meters come up just to "0." Keep in mind that in digital equipment (DAT, digital mixers, MDMs) the over indicator is just one step higher than the "0" indicator. If you cause it to light up, just reset it and adjust the input level slightly lower.

Now, the calibrated level tone should be appearing at the mixer's output. If you are using a desktop MDM, you can assign the signal to a record channel and verify that the metering at that point agrees. From the output of the mixer, you can feed the signal to other machines in your system, such as a computer workstation, DAT mixdown machine, or minidisc recorder. You can put these machines into record mode and adjust their input controls so that the recording meters read 0 dB. Leave them at this setting; some people like to place a paper marker on the level control so it can be repositioned if disturbed. Next, you can make a recording of this tone on tape (or hard disk), and then play it back to make sure the "in" and "out" levels agree. If playback levels don't match record levels within the machine, it needs a visit to Mr. Repair Technician for an internal tweak.

When setting up the calibrated "0" level on recording machines connected to a mixer, you can set the reference point at something other than "0" if you'd like. You can set up the recording machine to read a lower level (–12 dB and –18 dB are popular) while the mixer's meters read full-scale to provide an automatic cushion against over-levels. You can use this same basic procedure to set up cassette machines and verify the accuracy of left-right panning controls in your mixer (e.g., when a pan control is centered, both left and right meters of downstream machines should be equal).

Using these constant-level tones also shows up sneaky system faults, like flaky intermittent controls and bad interconnect cables. The tone should always show up on the meters as a rock-solid constant reading. If it fluctuates when you aren't changing anything, then you've found a problem that will ultimately show up in your recordings.

Don't be afraid to give this process a try, even if you are not too confident about doing these things. You will learn a lot about audio by going through these easy steps. Just remember to keep those monitors turned off!

The Ins and Outs of SMPTE
Timecode Unraveled
By David Darlington

What is timecode and why do you need it? If you're making music entirely within one piece of hardware or software, chances are that you don't need it at all. But if you're trying to make a drum machine's sequencer tag along to your computer's sequencer, or a workstation keyboard follow your taped vocal tracks, then you'll definitely need to understand and use timecode.

Linear timecode (LTC), the most common type of timecode used in professional music studios, is also called SMPTE ("SIMP-tee"), after the professional film union that standardized its format (the Society of Motion Picture and Television Engineers). When SMPTE timecode is recorded (or *striped*) onto a tape, it means that at any location on an audio track, there is a unique timecode address corresponding to it on an accompanying timecode track. This way, any machine that sees this address can "chase" to that point and synchronize with the first machine.

LTC comes in a few different flavors, defined by their frame rates since the code was originally developed to synchronize sound with film, which is divided into frames. The standard frame rate used in recording studios for audio is 30 frames per second (fps). Most devices that can read SMPTE display the code in a format indicating hours, minutes, seconds, and frames. For instance, a point three minutes and 30 seconds into a tape would generate 00:03:30:00 on a synchronizer's display.

With some MIDI interfaces, SMPTE can be generated from your computer by enabling the "timecode out" option. Most modular digital multitrack (MDM) controllers like the Alesis BRC or TASCAM DA-88 sync card can also generate it. Interestingly, MDMs can convert their digital tape locations into SMPTE by enabling an option in their software.

Another type of timecode is *MIDI timecode*, or MTC. MTC contains the same 30 fps address information as SMPTE, but is embedded in the MIDI data stream. This allows it to be sent from one machine to another with a simple MIDI cable. MTC out (or *send*) must be enabled on one machine, and MTC in (or *receive*) must be enabled on the other.

It's possible to use a combination of SMPTE and MTC. For example, on a TASCAM DA-88 recorder, the MIDI out of the sync card could feed the MIDI in of your drum machine, carrying MTC, while the SMPTE out could be routed to your MIDI interface's timecode in port. You must set each machine to look for the proper type of code and frame rate. These options are usually found under the Sync or External menu in sequencers and drum machines.

If your audio recorder is sending SMPTE to a sequencer and you want to use measures and beats as your time reference—as you would if creating songs—you must also program a tempo map in the sequencer and give the song an offset or starting point. On some machines this is called *song start*. Normally, on a tape, songs don't start in the same place (unless, for example, you're using 24-track tape and you use 12 tracks each for two songs) so you must tell your sequencer where to begin synching to the tape—at 00:00:00:00 or at 00:03:30:00, for example.

It's important to leave extra blank time between each song so that all of the machines have time to "chase" the master. If you begin a song right at 00:00:00:00, the master will start to play and the other machines will catch up somewhat later—not a great help when you're building a killer intro. I prefer 30 seconds of offset, meaning that my first song start will read 00:00:30:00. Some people use 20 seconds and some use even less. The more careful engineers I know allow for a full minute of offset "just in case." Of course, tape is notoriously fragile at the beginning and ending of a reel or cartridge, so the more time allowed, the merrier.

If you've set up everything correctly, then when you roll the tape and it reaches the 30-second mark, the sequencer or second tape machine will start to play at the same time in exactly the same tempo. Don't be discouraged if it doesn't work perfectly the first time. I've made a career out of troubleshooting timecode troubles. Just check all of your connections, software settings, and interfaces. If your studio is complex, try getting one machine to chase another and then add further devices one at a time. Once you've tamed the beast called SMPTE, it can make a wonderful pet.

Monitors and Monitoring

Output, Output, Output
The Bottom Line on Gear
By Rusty Cutchin

Everyone in New York knows how to get to Carnegie Hall, right? Practice, practice, practice. It's an old joke that can be turned around and applied to equipment. To paraphrase that old joke: How do you judge, a piece of gear? Output, output, output.

This is just a helpful way of remembering that the quality of the audio, image, or data that is ultimately produced by any piece of electronic gear is more important than the controls, looks, or even versatility of the piece. It's easy to understand, for example, that even if a refrigerator has a front-mounted ice-making system, side-by-side doors, a nuclear-powered thermostat, and a turkey sandwich replicator, it's useless if it doesn't keep the food cold. By the same token, a mixer may have 16 channels and parametric EQ, but if the Total Harmonic Distortion (THD) is 10 percent (an absurdly high number), it won't sound very good. If you got your microphones at a "buy one, get two free" sale, you can bet that their sonic output will not be as satisfying as that of a high-quality mic that costs a little more. If you cut costs or choose convenience by committing the final mix of your big project to cassette or MP3, the quality will have suffered to some degree because the outputs of these formats are inferior to CD-R, DAT, and even minidisc.

One of the first lessons a shopper learns in putting together a hi-fi system is that speakers should take up about half of the entire equipment budget. Why? Because without good monitors, the quality of the other components is wasted. The skills necessary to produce an accurate and dependable monitor system make these the most expensive elements in the chain. A successful engineer or producer has to maintain the quality of the work all the way through the recording process. If a piece of gear degrades the signal, the result will be obvious when the final product reaches its audience.

You might be surprised, in examining other media, how output quality is traded for convenience and speed. For example, most people agree that images captured on film are far richer and more detailed than those recorded on videotape. The producer creating the high-quality print, film, or audio versions of a work has to keep the data in near-perfect shape, so it will retain a certain level of quality when it winds up as a "low-res" copy.

Of course, audio formats seem to multiply like rabbits, and that state-of-the-art system you just bought may be replaced by a new design in a few months. As the "be the first on your block" crowd swarms to new technology, it becomes a challenge to keep your older gear producing comparable (and competitive) results while you look for a chance to upgrade. The important point should be that every piece of gear you buy should put out a signal that is at least as good as the one it is fed.

It takes training and experience to make judgments about output quality and it's usually accomplished by fine-tuning that great input device—your ears. Sometimes, even when you've examined the specs of a piece of gear, done your homework, and gotten lots of advice from other gearheads (ones with good input devices), the decision boils down to critical listening at a music store. Take advantage of the liberal (and reasonable) return policies of larger stores and bring the piece back if it doesn't sound good in your studio.

If you always take care to weed out the weak links in the recording chain, and make sure that every piece of gear you add (and maintain properly) outputs a signal as good or better than those they receive, then you will have a fine studio. You'll only have to worry about one other rule: "Garbage in, garbage out."

Subwoofer Strategies
Put Some Boom in Your Room
By David Darlington

One of the attractions of a pro recording studio is the large, usually incredibly loud, soffit-mounted monitor system with its imposing speakers. If you want to hear your record pump, these babies will make it happen. In the home recording environment, there just isn't enough room for gargantuan boxes, and the size of the room itself usually precludes moving enough air to feel that power. Often we have to be content with a pair of 8" or 10" drivers, which just don't reproduce real low-end frequencies, and also have a tendency to break up at high volume levels. If this is your lament, you may want to add a subwoofer to your monitor system. But before you go out and buy one and turn everything up to "11," however, there are a few points you should consider.

Adding a subwoofer to an existing system will have two results. The first and most obvious one is that the frequency range of the system will extend downward to include *subbass*—those frequencies below 70 Hz that most bookshelf monitors don't reproduce. The second is that the system will be apparently louder, because the subwoofer deals with those low frequencies that create large excursions in the main monitors, causing them to distort or crackle. With a subwoofer in the system, the mains are only dealing with 70 Hz and higher, give or take; therefore, they can output more volume before distorting. A subwoofer handles low frequencies easily, even at high output, because it doesn't need to reproduce mids and highs.

How does a subwoofer know which frequencies to play and which to pass? Typically the full-range L/R output of your console goes to a power amp and speakers, or to a pair of powered monitors that you control with the master fader or volume knob. When a subwoofer is incorporated into your system, the signal is sent first to the subwoofer where it passes through a circuit called a *crossover*. A crossover is a network that sends frequencies below a certain value to one output and frequencies above that value to another. The dividing frequency is called the *crossover point*, and it is usually adjustable. Most subwoofers allow you to adjust the crossover point on the rear panel where the other connections are made. With this setup, your volume control is really controlling the input of the crossover, and the crossover is controlling the outputs to the mains and subwoofer. Setting the crossover point is critical to getting the most out of your system. If the frequency is set too low, not enough energy will come from the sub and too much will go to the mains. If the frequency is set too high, the subwoofer will receive too much energy and the mains won't get enough, resulting in a dark or boomy sound. The crossover point is usually between 50 Hz and 100 Hz—about 75 or 80 Hz for most home studio systems. You must fine-tune the crossover point by ear until your speakers are operating as efficiently as possible.

A subwoofer's level control is also important. Since the sub has its own amplifier, its volume is independent of the main speakers. Adjusting the volume on the subwoofer regulates the level of low frequencies relative to the mids and highs. Here is where most home studios run into trouble: You want your room to pump, but more importantly you want the monitors to be true. If you set the subwoofer level too high, you may be fooled into thinking that your mixes have great bottom, when in fact the bottom is coming from the subwoofer and not your mix. Conversely, if it is set too low, you won't hear enough low-frequency content (or undesirable low-end material that you need to eliminate) in your monitors, so you might overemphasize these frequencies in your mix.

The point to keep in mind is that you're trying to enhance the listening environment, not hype it. With the right fine-tuning, your system can be loud and pumping and yet remain accurate for monitoring purposes. Check your mixes in as many places as possible, and don't rest until your subwoofer is tweaked out and set perfectly. Then sit back and enjoy that pumped-up bass.

Monitoring 101
Creating a Quality Monitoring Environment—Part 1 of 3
By Pat Kirtley

Cruising through the pages of recording and music magazines these days, I see lots of pictures of home and project studios with smiling owner/mixer/producer/musician types sitting amid racks and stacks of quality gear. But one thing I keep noticing in these photos (including those of—sorry, folks—most of the studios profiled in this very magazine) is that monitor speakers are rarely set up as intended by their designers, and that mixing rooms have been laid out with little regard for the laws of acoustics. No wonder you guys are having a hard time getting reliable mixes! To improve this situation, we need to get straight with Mother Nature and start applying the basic acoustic principles that have been known in the pro audio world for more than 50 years.

This series of three articles is about creating your own quality monitoring environment. The concept is straightforward: Choose the right speakers, place them correctly in the listening environment, and eliminate some major room problems. If you do all of this, you will be far ahead of the game in creating a good studio monitoring system. Your monitor system does not consist of just the speakers, the room, or the acoustic treatments used in the room—it is rather an interactive combination of all three. Using the principles shown in this series, you will be able to evaluate your current listening setup and make significant improvements in the quality of your recording work.

The room in which you do your monitoring and mixing is part of the audio playback system, just as much as any processor or EQ device. The room is a *huge* factor that won't go away by itself. While listening with loudspeakers, you are always "hearing" the room you are in, and it is almost never a room designed for the optimal playback of music through speakers, especially if it's a room in your home. Even a room that sounds great with live musicians degrades the performance of a playback system dramatically. For mixing and monitoring, you need the room to work together with the speakers, not fight them. There are companies that make a living applying the science of room design and speaker positioning to create highly functional monitoring and mixing environments. The services of these audio geniuses are priced out of the range of most project studio owners, but the basic principles of control room design and monitor placement can be utilized by anyone who wants to spend the time to understand the basic laws of acoustics.

Monitors Defined

What makes a speaker a "monitor"? There are lots of great speakers available from scores of manufacturers. The special qualities that define a speaker system as a monitor are extended frequency response, low distortion, and rugged power-handling characteristics. Such qualities are found in other speaker types—low distortion and extended frequency response in quality hi-fi speakers, and high-power handling in PA speaker systems—but a studio monitor demands the presence of all three qualities. It makes these speakers more difficult to design and manufacture, and it's the reason good monitors tend to be some of the most expensive speakers you can buy.

Neophyte recordists often wonder, "Why can't I just use a good pair of hi-fi speakers for monitors?" Well, you might get away with it. There have been numerous great speaker designs in the hi-fi world over the years, but in the last 20 years or so there has been a disturbing trend toward hi-fi speakers designed to sound "attractive." They have an extra dose of bass response and/or some serious high-end sparkle, and in casual listening you might like these effects. But too much bass in a monitoring environment causes the mixing engineer to cut back on the low end, yielding an anemic music mix that sounds good only on similarly hyped speakers. The same goes for speakers with hot treble, blatant mids, bipolar dispersion, or whatever the design-of-the-week club comes up with. A good monitor speaker's frequency response is even, accurate, and dependably neutral. It is less exciting, I suppose, in the way that a commuter train is less exciting than a sports car. They both move people around, but while the sports car is a thrill to experience, the train can be counted on to get us where we're going in a safe and reliable manner, time and again.

Another serious area where hi-fi speaker designs fall short as monitors is in power-handling capacity. Studio monitors get abused on a regular basis, with audio sources thrown at them that hi-fi speakers were never designed to handle, such as ten minutes of sustained high-level kick drum tweaking, or the errant high-volume synth sine wave resulting from someone's elbow accidentally resting on a keyboard. Hi-fi speakers were designed to pass nice, clean, fully formed mixes, and when blasted with the raw-audio generated during the recording process, they have a tendency to self-destruct. Try using your hi-fi speakers as monitors, and you will learn all of these things firsthand. Or get way ahead of the game and buy real monitor speakers.

Classes of Monitors

There are several categories of studio monitors, and your control room may feature one or more of them.

Large monitors are known as a *primary reference*, and in many cases will be permanently mounted at some distance from the console position. Typically, they feature bass drivers in the range of 10" to 15". In the big pro studios, these monitors are often mounted inside a wall or overhead soffit with just the front face showing. In many cases, the primary monitors are considered so important that the rest of the studio is designed around them. *Near-field monitors* face the engineer from a much closer distance and usually serve the function of *secondary reference*. Typically they have bass drivers in the 5" to 8" range, and are positioned at the back edge of the console area, 3" to 5" from the engineer's head. In home studios, such speakers will often be the only (and hence primary reference) monitoring system.

Miniature monitors have bass drivers in the 3" to 4" range (sometimes without treble drivers at all) and function in the studio world as a compromised reference. They serve to let us know what a mix will sound like on a clock radio or small TV speaker where, like it or not, lots of consumer listening is done.

Personal monitors, otherwise known as headphones, serve well in the mixing and monitoring process by providing yet another perspective on a mix. Though they give an exaggerated and unnatural stereo image, when you have to work in proximity to other people and not bother them, headphones often must serve on a temporary basis as primary monitors.

Design Types

Beyond the size issue, there are several different designs of monitor speakers. By far most common are those based on ported cabinets. There is always a trade-off in the low frequency ranges between efficiency and extended bass response. In general, a cabinet that is totally sealed allows for a flatter and more extended frequency response in the low end, but less maximum volume. A ported design has one or more openings that allow airflow from the back of the bass speaker cone to reach the outside of the cabinet. This allows more freedom of movement for the speaker cone, thus raising efficiency, but it also raises the lowest frequency that can be reproduced. In today's designs, speaker engineers have achieved a good tradeoff between efficiency and low-end response, and even speakers with large drivers (12" and larger) are ported designs.

A factor that becomes important is the location of the *port(s)*. You can always see them—they're the round holes in the cabinet, either on the front or the back. It becomes problematic when you need to place a speaker flush against a wall, and find that in doing so you would block a rear-firing port. Blocking ports, as you might imagine, causes a significant change in the performance of the speaker (though for various sonic reasons you might sometimes *want* to do this).

Another type of design found in current speakers like the Mackie HR824 uses something called a *passive radiator*. This is an un-driven speaker cone that is used to translate vibrations from the woofer to the outside air in a controlled way, and performs a function somewhat like a port. These passive radiator devices, which look much like another woofer cone, are often found on the rear (or sides) of the cabinet, and must not be blocked by inappropriate speaker placement.

Let Me Count the Ways . . .

No one speaker driver can efficiently cover the entire audio range. It usually takes at least two drivers—a large *woofer* for bass with response extending into the upper midrange frequencies, and a *tweeter,* which handles the upper mid, extending up to the highest audible frequencies. Speakers with a woofer and tweeter are called *two-way designs,* and require circuitry ahead of the drivers—called a *crossover*—to divide the incoming audio into the appropriate frequency range for each driver.

If you want a speaker to play very loud and to be able to go down to the lowest audio frequencies, the bass driver should be pretty large. At diameters of 10" and greater, a bass driver gets progressively worse at reproducing mid-range frequencies. In such speakers, a third driver, specialized for mid-range operation, is added. This speaker system is called a *three-way*, and requires a more complex crossover system. There are also a few four-way speaker designs, typically with drivers designated as woofer, *low-mid driver, mid driver,* and tweeter. Some designers also double up on the drivers—typically using two woofers instead of one—for added dynamic range and power-handling capacity.

In the last few years, another design type has emerged. There are now lots of multi-unit speaker systems that feature two smallish cabinets, each with a tweeter and small midrange/woofer. A third cabinet contains a subwoofer (sometimes the third cabinet should be more accurately labeled simply "woofer"). The idea here stems from the fact that bass frequencies below about 100 Hz—roughly the pitch of the open A string on a guitar—are omnidirectional, and the ear cannot localize the direction from which they originate. Therefore, speaker designers reasoned, why not put the bulky woof box somewhere out of sight, and have just two unobtrusive little boxes in front of the listener. Some of these designs are interesting, but in a monitoring environment the idea tends to be problematic. Mainly, it's hard to find a place to put a subwoofer that will give consistent bass output throughout the room. These systems also sometimes suffer from a very strange frequency response anomaly at the point where the sound transfers from the little boxes to the subwoofer, owing to the distance displacement between the drivers. In general, using three-piece mid/high subwoofer systems for control-room monitoring and achieving the correct setup is difficult.

Passive vs. Active Monitors

One of the most amazing recent developments in the monitor speaker world is the *active* or *powered monitor*. This concept eliminates so many potential problems that it's strange that we didn't come up with it sooner. Actually, it took a significant amount of computer-aided design and engineering effort to make the concept work. The complexity of the task is the same reason why we didn't have carbon-fiber composite airplane wings in the 1950s—the materials were there, but we hadn't figured out how to put them together yet.

The active monitor system is an engineering triumph—the amplifiers are contained in the speakers. You don't have to have an extra component (i.e., the power amp) cluttering up your studio. More important, the ever-problematic issue of speaker cabling is virtually eliminated since signals go into each monitor at line level. Now, the speaker cables are completely internal and just a couple of inches in length. And since the speakers are right next to the electronics, designers can include such niceties as electronic overload sensing and speaker protection for little extra cost. It's also more cost effective to design these systems with hi-amplified electronic crossovers instead of the less accurate passive variety. The active monitors might seem expensive until you realize all you are getting for one price. Before long, they will probably dominate the project studio monitor market.

On the other hand, if you already own a beefy, high-quality amplifier, there are plenty of good passive monitor designs available. Especially for small near-field monitors, the design of passive two-way systems is mature, and many monitors even in the lower price ranges have good performance.

At the upper end of monitor design are those systems featuring not only active design, but also the ability to accept a digital audio signal as input. It's a great concept, but at present not fully matured. Digital standards are still changing, and you might find two years later that you have a great set of speakers that won't "talk to" some new console or other piece of equipment you have acquired. Still, as long as the digital-ready speaker also includes a line-level analog input, you can purchase without fear of creeping obsolescence.

Pros and Cons

One important decision is the choice of which type of monitor to use for your monitoring environment. If you have a fairly large space and want to listen at very loud levels, you need large speakers and the big amp channels they require. Big drivers can move more air—it's as simple as that.

Big drivers can also reproduce lower frequencies than smaller ones. This goes back to basic audio physics, but audio physics also permits smaller drivers to reproduce low bass frequencies if the volume requirements are scaled back. This fact accounts for the extreme success of small near-field monitors. If you don't have to move much air, you can reproduce low bass frequencies even with a tiny driver (think headphones). So, the trade-offs are always volume level vs. decreasing driver size vs. extended bass response. You can maximize any one of these in a small speaker, but not all three. That's fine in the case of near-field monitors, and explains their success.

Positioned close to the ears of an engineer, near-field monitors sound louder by virtue of proximity. The designers may also choose to enhance the efficiency by using a ported design, which increases the output of the woofer, but at the expense of response in the low-bass region. What we end up with is a speaker with a 5" to 8" low-frequency driver that can do everything except play very loudly and produce deep, thundering bass. It's a workable trade-off. When the speaker is close to your ears (typically 3' to 4'), the volume level produced can be plenty loud for most purposes.

If you choose to go with large format monitors, they must be placed further from the mixing position. They have, in addition to a more impressive "oomph" factor, the advantage of allowing more listeners to be in the *sweet spot*—where the sound is most balanced. They also require seriously larger amplifiers than those required by near-field speakers.

One way of looking at using big monitors as opposed to near-fields is to make a cost comparison. If a quality pair of near-fields and associated amplifiers costs $1,000, you can expect to pay around $4,000 for an equivalent large monitor setup. The big commercial studios, of course, like to have both types of systems in place.

A good compromise between the commanding qualities of leviathan permanent monitors and the lower-cost, less problematic mini near-fields would be one of the larger near-field monitor designs with bass drivers in the 8" range. These monitors throw a healthy punch and can produce nearly flat bass response down to around 40 Hz or so. The good ones aren't exactly cheap, but this is one area of studio spending that truly can be a long-term investment.

Speakers (and mics) are the studio items least affected by technological obsolescence. As you will see in the coming installments of this series, there are lots of reasons why many home/project studios are at their best with the near-field solution.

Monitoring 101
Creating a Quality Monitoring Environment—Part 2 of 3
By Pat Kirtley

Rooms and Speaker Placement

If you could invite a world-class studio designer into your own studio for a quick evaluation, you might hear this: "Your speakers are fine but the acoustic environment really sucks." In the pro-studio world, mixing rooms are often literally designed around the speakers, with the ultimate expense of doing it that way taken for granted. Home recordists are seldom lucky (or rich) enough to benefit from such a no-compromise approach to acoustic design. More likely you will squeeze your audio work environment into some space otherwise unoccupied by the necessities of daily living. This space will significantly compromise the performance of your monitor speakers unless you do something to get the laws of acoustics working on your side. The objective here is to get monitor speakers to function well in typical rooms.

Speaker performance is *always* affected by the room. Speaker manufacturers design and measure the performance of their products using a baseline acoustic space called an *anechoic chamber*. This special measuring space is designed to be as close as possible to acoustic nothingness—a virtual sonic black hole that absorbs all sound. It is necessary for designers to make anechoic measurements to remove the room from the equation. They know that it's impossible to predict the characteristics of the room in which the speaker will ultimately be used. For the aspiring home recordist/project engineer, selecting and preparing a workable acoustic environment is a critical task.

One Space Fits All

The home recording revolution has popularized the use of a single space for all audio purposes—live recording, vocal and instrumental overdubbing, playback monitoring, and mixing. To many home recordists, the basic pro-studio concept of separate control room and studio space seems foreign, and the all-in-one room idea offers some refreshing simplicities. Costly and difficult isolation between studio and control room becomes a non-factor, and you need no special communication system among engineer, producer, and performers.

An obvious problem is that there can be no real-time judgment of what's actually being recorded while the recording is in progress because the live performers and the mics are in the same space as the monitoring system. A workable compromise for many home recordists is to use one room as a control and monitoring space, and another room—sometimes at a considerable distance—for the live recording space. One or more small and inexpensive TV cameras (or camcorders without tape running) provide visual contact between performer and engineer. The focus of this article is on rooms used as monitoring and mixing spaces, with only secondary thought given to using them for live recording. However, an acoustically well-controlled listening space is generally suitable for live recording, too.

The laws of acoustics are complex, and they govern the performance of every monitoring environment. Most of us will never have the need to master the science of acoustics, but there are great benefits to be derived from knowledge of the basics. It's time to look at some simplified laws of acoustics as they apply to speakers and listening rooms.

The Three Rs of Acoustics

The sonic quirks of typical rooms stand in the way of creating a first-rate audio workspace. Real-life rooms—the ones in which you are likely to install your studio—come in various dimensional proportions, and need help to become good monitoring spaces. Along with helping the room, you need an intelligent strategy for speaker placement. To understand how a room affects speaker performance, it is worthwhile to learn a few basic principles of acoustics. For one, rooms have three acoustic "Rs": *resonance, reflectivity*, and *reverberation*.

Resonance is a room characteristic that causes particular frequencies to be increased in intensity based on the dimensions and shape of the room. The most severe resonance modes are those of the worst rooms—small, straight-sided, and rectangular, a.k.a. the kind most commonly found in typical homes. The distance between two parallel walls determines the frequency that will be emphasized by resonance. The phenomenon of resonance is easily demonstrated by blowing air across the top of a soft drink bottle. The pitch of the resulting pure tone is determined by the strongest resonance mode of this enclosed space. A cylindrical enclosure (the approximate shape of a bottle) has one major resonance mode, and hence one note, but rectangular rooms have *three* major modes.

Each dimension of a room—length, depth, and height—is responsible for emphasizing a specific frequency. For a typical "spare bedroom" of say, 10'x13'x8', the strongest resonances are in the mid-bass range—say, 60 to 200 Hz. When a speaker vibrates the air in a room at a resonant frequency, the energy is boosted by the resonance mode, and sound at that frequency becomes louder. Also, resonance modes excite the harmonics of the basic frequency. For a 60 Hz fundamental resonance, the harmonics appear at even intervals of 120, 240, 480 Hz, and so on. Take the three basic frequencies associated with the length, width, and height dimensions, imagine the interplay of the basic frequencies and all of the harmonics, and you can see the complexity of trying to control room resonance.

Reflectivity is the ability of an object or a surface to reflect sound waves; this is the dominant room characteristic affecting the mid and treble ranges. *Absorption*, the opposite of reflection, is the ability of an object or a surface to stop the travel of sound waves to some degree. Smooth, hard surfaces are highly reflective, whereas soft, porous objects such as stuffed, cloth-upholstered furniture are highly absorptive. In case you are wondering, bass frequencies are reflected and absorbed, too, but not by the same physical characteristics that affect mids and highs. Intelligent speaker-locating strategies seek to avoid the worst effects of bass reflectivity by placing speakers at specific distances from walls, or flush against them.

Reverberation is a characteristic present in rooms of all sizes—not just churches and gymnasiums—and it exists because sound bounces between reflective surfaces not just once, but repeatedly until the last bit of it weakens and dies. As a sound re-reflects and diminishes, it is affected by nearly every object and surface in a room. In small rooms the *decay time* (i.e., how long it takes a sound to die away) can be very short—much less than one second—but reverberation always affects your subjective impression of how a room sounds.

As sound dies away and is affected by every surface in a room, it quickly becomes *incoherent*—a term that in acoustics parlance means "all blended together." But the first reflections of mid- and high-frequency sound get bounced back to our ears in a way that is quite coherent if there are hard objects and surfaces near the sound's direct path. These slightly delayed first-order reflections can cause big problems because they affect our impression of the stereo sound field as well as our impressions of delicate, short-term sounds (think of the attacks of ride cymbals and hi-hats, for instance). In the world of acoustics, though first reflections are part of the process called *reverb*, we treat the two characteristics as if they were unique phenomena.

The Most Basic Speaker Positioning Idea

The basic rule: When positioning speakers, consider the low-frequency performance factors first.

How speakers are affected by the low-frequency modes of a room is a critical factor. In typical small rooms, most of the mid- and high-frequency problems of reflectivity and reverberation can be corrected, but low-end room resonances present another difficulty. A frustrating effect you may have noticed in a monitoring environment is that the apparent amount of bass varies as you move around the room; it is much less in some spots and greater in others. Just by moving to different places in the room, you can get an effect that sounds like someone is turning the bass control up and down. In many rooms, you may notice a large increase in low-end energy as your head gets near the back wall at the furthest point from the speakers. To deal with this problem, you need to know how speakers interact with the room in the bass region.

Speaker designers talk about "acoustic space" in terms of speaker placement in relation to room boundaries (ceiling, walls, and floor). They have designated three basic "spaces." *Full space* describes the environment of a speaker surrounded on all sides by free air, and not near any wall, ceiling, or floor surface. A speaker mounted on a 3' pedestal stand would be considered to be in full space.

Half space is when a speaker is bounded by one wall surface. If you take the same speaker position as above and move the speaker and pedestal stand so that the speaker's back is flat against the wall, the speaker is operating in half space. In this configuration, bass response from about 50 Hz or so on down increases by around 3 to 6 dB, relative to the speaker in full space. Speakers mounted flush inside a wall so that the front of the speaker cabinet is even with the wall surface are also operating in half space.

Quarter space describes corner speaker placement. This configuration creates a low-end response increase of around 6 to 8 dB. A fourth "space," and one that is not usually considered workable for speaker placement, is *eighth space*, which describes a speaker on the floor in a corner, or at the ceiling in a corner. Bass output is increased even more in this case, up to 12 dB compared with full space.

We can predict, with reasonable accuracy, how a speaker will perform when positioned in the above-mentioned configurations. Problems arise when a speaker is not right up against a wide, flat surface, but is instead positioned some distance away. Bass frequencies always interact with nearby surfaces; the resulting problem, called *low-frequency cancellation*, can occur when a speaker cabinet is within a few feet of a wall surface. Room resonances cause certain bass frequencies to be emphasized, but low-frequency cancellation causes certain frequencies to be drastically reduced in level. While room resonance can be hard to control, cancellation problems can be managed by correct speaker placement.

The Concept of Near-Field Monitoring

Within the last 20 or so years, studio engineers and speaker designers have been exploring a concept called *near-field monitoring*. Near-field monitoring solves many room problems simply by placing the speakers closer to the ears of the listener. Typically, the distance from the speaker to the engineer's ears is about 3' to 4'. The idea behind near-field monitoring is to minimize negative room qualities by getting a greater proportion of direct speaker sound than reflected sound. The more your ears hear the sound from the speakers themselves and the less they hear the room's imperfections, the closer the sound delivery is to the way the manufacturer designed the speaker.

Getting rid of a room is not simple, however. Speakers operate over a range of frequencies that interact with a room in radically different ways. Speaker positioning decisions are based on trade-offs among a number of factors. It is important to remember that near-field monitoring is an approach that *minimizes* room-interaction problems, but does not *eliminate* them.

Near-Field Positioning

To visualize the factors involved, one can consider the total frequency range of a loud-speaker to be divided into three ranges: low end (approximately 20 to 200 Hz), mids (200 to 2,000 Hz), and highs (2,000 to 20,000 Hz). Each range has its own factors that are addressed by the near-field approach.

Low-end room interactions are minimized in near-field monitoring by keeping the speakers away from room boundaries. A distance of at least 3' is required to avoid unpredictable response at the lowest frequencies. It is also desirable to have no two equal distances between the speaker and closest room boundaries. For instance, don't position a speaker on 4' pedestals exactly 4' out from the back wall. In effect, that location allows the same low frequency to be reinforced or cancelled twice. For the same reasons, don't put a speaker on a pedestal that's exactly 4' high in a room with an 8' ceiling. For near-field monitor performance in the bass range, unequal distancing from nearby room boundaries is the way to go. The unequal lengths need not be radical: 3 1/2' from a back wall and 4' off the floor, for instance, should be adequate to avoid the worst low-end problems.

This positioning approach is difficult to apply to very small rooms. Giving up 3' of space by putting your mixer table and speakers that far out from the wall might result in an uncomfortably cramped workspace. In that case, consider the alternative of putting the speakers flush against the back wall. The thing to avoid is having a small space (less than 3') between the wall and the speaker. Put the speakers either well away from the wall or right on it.

The considerations for high frequencies (about 2,000 to 20,000 Hz) focus on reflections from nearby surfaces between the front of the speaker and the listener's ears. Here, the distance between the speakers and the side walls as well as other objects and surfaces in the speakers' "field of view" should be considered. When working out speaker positioning in terms of high frequencies, it is important to consider the relative distances between the speaker, the listener's ears, and nearby surfaces. The idea is to have a much greater amount of direct sound coming toward you than reflected from surfaces. It follows that surfaces very close to the speaker are important, such as the flat surface of the mixer board, the front of a large video monitor, or nearby racks of outboard gear. The ideal setup would be just two speakers floating in the air in front of you, relatively far from the room walls and with no nearby surfaces between you and the speakers. Since that scenario only exists in some fantasy listening showroom, there are always real situations you must evaluate in your own monitoring environment.

In terms of speaker placement, mid-frequencies (200 to 2,000 Hz) will generally fall into line if you address the low- and high-frequency factors correctly. This it not to say that you won't have problems that affect the mid-frequencies, but there isn't much you can do about them with speaker placement.

Symmetry and Non-Symmetry

Symmetry is the quality of similarity in two directions. The important axis of symmetry in monitor-speaker placement is an imaginary vertical plane extending from the middle of the listener's head outward. The side room walls and speakers should be at equal distances on either side of this line. In other words, it's ideal to have the mixing board and speaker setup centered horizontally in the room, and not up against a corner.

It is also desirable to have the speakers arranged in a mirror-image pattern—usually with the tweeter on top of the woofer in small two-way designs—though this symmetry isn't as important as the side-to-side positioning symmetry. This midline mirror-image symmetry has been emphasized by speaker designers because it helps to create good stereo imaging.

A perfect stereo image is a sound field in which you can pick out the precise horizontal position of panned sound sources in a mix. The quest for perfection in stereo imaging can be a dangerous trap for the recordist. It is not that difficult to achieve good imaging, especially with near-field monitoring. The problem is that after you've attained near-perfection mix imaging, it's easy to get sucked into this seductive aspect of the sound field—and most of your consumers in typical listening environments can't re-create it. Many consumer listening environments are essentially monophonic, though the sound source is two-channel stereo. Don't spend too much time fussing with this aspect of speaker setup.

A place where you don't need symmetry or sameness is in the overall measurements of the room. Problematic rooms tend to be those with evenly divisible proportions, such as 12'x16'x8' (all dimensions evenly divisible by four). The worst kind of room for audio monitoring is a square box with all sides equal—for instance, 8'x8'x8'. Better rooms are those with dissimilar (i.e., not evenly divisible) dimensions of length, width, and height. A workable room might be one with measurements of 11'x7'x8'. Even better are rooms with nonparallel walls. Sloping ceilings are good, and sometimes you can find an attic space where the walls follow the contour of the roof, are broken up by dormers, etc., to be a wonderful acoustic space.

Go for It

You can't just stick your speakers in some likely location and hope for the best. Experimenting with locations to see what sounds best might be okay for a casual listening situation, but it won't help in setting up monitors. No matter how your audio workspace is currently laid out, try rethinking it according to the ideas presented here. Remember that the ultimate goal is to hear things properly from your monitors, so that your mixing decisions and balances will play properly on a variety of playback systems, from audiophile setups to car stereos to boom boxes and TV speakers.

We will next look at ways to use acoustic materials—both everyday materials and specialized acoustic products—to correct specific room problems, and show you how to achieve professional monitoring performance even in the most problematic acoustic spaces.

Room Tips for Monitoring Setup

- Try to choose a room that is large enough to allow for the proper placement of near-field monitors. The necessary gap between the front wall and your speakers takes up a lot of room.

- If your room is small (less than 10'x10'x8'), consider putting the speakers directly against the wall, or even mounting them flush into the wall so that only the front faces show. Doing this requires compensating for the extra low-frequency output; follow the speaker manufacturer's guidelines precisely when using these placement methods.

- Remember to follow the concept of vertical midline symmetry when deciding on speaker placement. Avoid nonsymmetrical placements of equipment racks or other flat surfaces near the speakers.

- Pristine stereo imaging is great, but don't put too much emphasis on achieving it. Good mixes depend on getting a balance of all of the sound sources. A vivid stereo field sounds great, but it can seduce your attention away from that primary goal. Few end-product listeners pay much attention to stereo imaging.

- Try to set up your mixing area so it's centered on the shortest side of a rectangular room. In the case of a 12'x16' room, this would mean near the center of the 12' end.

- Avoid setting up a mixing area in a corner.

- Odd-shaped rooms (L-shapes, or rooms with large openings into another space) are okay, but try to find a position along the shortest wall for the mixing area.

- Try to position the monitors at ear level and aimed inward toward the listener's head. However, don't be obsessive about the need for inward aiming. If the speakers are aimed flat toward the room or just slightly inward, more than one listener can take advantage of the sweet spot where good imaging occurs.

Speaker Positioning Axioms

- Remember that putting speakers near walls increases bass output. If it is necessary to position them this way, follow the manufacturer's guidelines to reduce bass output by precisely measured amounts. This may include setting control switches on the speaker cabinets, partially blocking portholes, or adjusting active crossover levels.

- Most near-field monitors are designed to deliver their most accurate performance in free air, well away from room boundaries.

- Don't put two speakers of a stereo pair in two different acoustic spaces, (i.e., avoid putting one speaker in a corner and one in free space).

Idiot Check

When hooking up your monitor system, make absolutely certain that your speakers are in phase with each other. You can assure this by carefully following the plus (+) and minus (–) terminal designations and color codes on speaker wiring. If the speakers are out of phase, they will still work, but the audio performance will suffer drastically. One test for proper in-phase operation is to play a monophonic source through the system (i.e., an identical signal going to both speakers). If the speakers are in phase, you will hear the sound image appearing to come from neither speaker, but from a distinct spot midway between the two.

A Glossary of Room Acoustics Terms

Anechoic Chamber: A room designed to absorb sound at all frequencies. It is used only for acoustical measurements and testing.

Audible Frequency Range: Audio frequencies that are audible vary from person to person, and in the average person, the upper limit of audible frequencies gets lower with age. A child with normal hearing might be able to perceive tones with a frequency of near 20 kHz, but most people older than age 30 cannot hear frequencies higher than about 15 kHz.

Audio Frequency: An acoustical or electrical signal of a frequency within the audible range of human hearing, usually defined as 20 Hz to 20 kHz.

Bass Frequencies: The lower range of audible frequencies, approximately 20 to 200 Hz.

Coloration: In describing room acoustics, the alteration of tonal quality caused by undesirable room characteristics. Coloration can be minimized by proper speaker placement and by applying acoustic treatments to a room.

Decay Time: The time it takes for sound to die away in a room. Typically, it is less than half a second for small, residential rooms.

Echo: A sound wave that has been reflected by a surface or object with sufficient delay time (typically 90 milliseconds or greater) to be perceived as distinct from the original sound. Discrete reflections returning at times shorter than approximately 50 ms blend with the original and are perceived by humans as tone coloration changes rather than separate sounds.

Flush Mounting: The placement of speakers inside a wall or other structure so that just the front face of the enclosure is visible. The purpose of flush mounting is to eliminate the problems caused by the reflection of bass frequencies from nearby walls.

Flutter Echo: In room acoustics, a series of specific reflective returns caused by large surfaces being parallel to each other. Clapping your hands in a totally empty room will give you an example of how a flutter echo sounds.

Free-Space Mounting: The positioning of monitor speakers away from any room boundaries. An example is mounting speakers on a narrow pedestal, or hanging them by chains or wires from a ceiling. Effectively, the speaker is hanging in midair, and low frequencies are propagated omnidirectionally.

Harmonic: In acoustics, a sound wave that is a multiple of the original frequency. For example, 200 Hz is the frequency of the first harmonic of a 100 Hz frequency wave. The base frequency (i.e., 100 Hz) is called a *fundamental*.

Hertz (Hz): A term expressing the frequency of a wave or signal. One Hertz is one cycle per second; 2,000 Hertz equals 2,000 cycles per second. kHz means kilohertz or Hz times 1,000; 10 kHz=10,000 Hz. Sometimes kHz is further abbreviated as simply "k." The Hertz is named in honor of electronics and physics pioneer Heinrich Hertz.

High Frequencies: The upper range of audible frequencies (approximately 2,000 Hz to 20,000 Hz).

Imaging: The ability of a stereo monitoring system to create the illusion of multiple sound sources appearing at various points horizontally between the two speakers. In a playback environment with good imaging, panned instruments or vocals in a mix seem to be distinctly resolved points in space. With bad imaging, the audible images seem horizontally smeared and indistinct.

Mid Frequencies: The middle range of audible frequencies (approximately 200 Hz to 2000 Hz).

Mode: Room resonance. Axial modes are associated with pairs of parallel walls. Tangential modes involve four room surfaces; oblique modes involve six surfaces. Their effect is greatest at low frequencies and for small rooms.

Near-Field Monitor: A speaker system designed to operate with flat frequency response while positioned away from walls or other room boundaries. It is also designed to be placed relatively close to the listener's ears. The basic idea is to have a greater proportion of direct sound from the speakers reaching the listener's ears than secondarily reflected sounds from the room.

Phase: The time relationship between two waves or signals. In acoustics, phase usually refers to the relationship of two sound waves that interact in some way, either *in-phase* (energies added together), *out-of-phase* (energies subtracted), or somewhere between the two extremes.

Polarity: In speakers and microphones, the relationship between the plus (+) and minus (–) connections and the equipment to which the devices are connected. For stereo monitor speaker pairs, it is critically important that both speakers be connected in an identical way from the terminals on the back of the amplifier to the terminals on the back of the speakers (i.e., always plus-to-plus and minus-to-minus). If you don't follow the proper connection procedure, the speakers' signals will be out of phase (see **Phase**), and performance will suffer dramatically.

Resonance: The ability of an object or physical space to sustain or emphasize a particular frequency. In musical instruments, resonance is a good thing, but in reproduction systems and rooms, resonance is detrimental, and we as engineers should attempt to reduce its effects in various ways.

Reverberation: Sound waves continue to bounce around surfaces and objects in a room until their energy is dissipated. In room acoustics, reverberation refers to sound that persists after a tone is suddenly stopped. A room that is noticeably reverberant is called *live* (or sometimes, for larger spaces, *wet*). A room that is not very reverberant is called *dead* or *dry*. The two main qualities of reverberation are quantity ("liveness") and length (reverberation time). All normal rooms have reverberation.

Reverberation Time: The length of time sound persists in a room after the original sound source stops. In the field of acoustics, it is defined as the time required for the sound in a room to drop 60 dB. This figure was agreed upon by acoustics engineers so that they could create a universal measurement standard. You will sometimes see this term abbreviated as RT60.

Room Resonances (also called Room Modes): Frequencies at which sound waves in a room resonate (in the form of standing waves), based on the room dimensions. Acoustics experts have defined several specific modes (i.e., tangential, axial, oblique) to describe typical rooms based on the various ways that sound interacts with the room surfaces. The most basic concept is that room mode is determined by the dimensions of the room.

Soffit Mounting: Flush-mounting of speakers into an overhead structure built out away from the original wall in a room. A soffit usually runs across the entire length of a wall.

Sound Waves: The alternating compression and expansion of a medium through which sounds travel. The typical medium is air. Frequency determines the length of the waves, and amplitude or volume determines the strength of the waves. At 20 Hz (the lowest audible frequency), the wavelength is about 54'. At 20 kHz (highest frequency audible by the best ears), the wavelength is .05'.

Standing Wave: In acoustics, an apparently stationary waveform created by multiple reflections between opposite room surfaces. At certain points along the standing wave, the direct and reflected waves cancel, and at other points the waves add together or reinforce each other. In typical residential-size rooms, standing wave problems occur at bass frequencies.

Wavelength: The distance a sound wave travels during one cycle. The distance between one peak or crest of a sine wave and the next corresponding peak or crest. The wavelength of any frequency may be found by dividing the speed of sound by the frequency. (The speed of sound at sea level is 331.4 meters/second or 1087.42 feet/second.)

Monitoring 101
Creating a Quality Monitoring Environment—Part 3 of 3
By Pat Kirtley

Acoustic Room Treatments

Once you've chosen good quality monitor speakers, found a reasonably good room for setting up a playback space, and decided on speaker location, upgrading your workspace to a high-quality mixing and monitoring environment will require further thought and effort. Every interior space you are likely to encounter is imperfect for audio use, and some spaces are worse than others. We've already examined speaker selection and basic room acoustics. The third piece of the acoustic environment puzzle is room treatment, and this article will explore the ways in which you can use materials (both common, everyday materials and specialized acoustic products), to refine your monitoring room so it sounds (and looks) great.

Before we proceed, here is a disclaimer about the intent of this article. Studio acoustic construction and treatment is a complex field. You will note that we are focusing here on using existing rooms, and don't delve into the construction and remodeling concepts used to create studio spaces. Studio construction, whether it involves building from the ground up or revamping interior spaces, is its own topic, and we couldn't do justice to it within the scope of this article. Acoustic isolation, another important aspect of studio design not covered here, also demands its own treatment.

The Objective

Never lose sight of the primary goal when setting up a listening environment. Our hard-headed objective is to make recordings and mixes the best we can. In doing room treatments, we simply seek to eliminate things that stand in the way of making great recordings. There have been many philosophies over the years regarding ways to set up monitoring environments, so it is easy to be misled by the conflicting theories championed by various experts. The recommendations we give here are generally accepted ones. We'll ignore the "audio boutique theories" that seem to gain currency and then fade away after a couple of years.

Back in the 1960s, designers started making audio control rooms as "dead" as possible, with the idea that, as you killed sound reflection at all frequencies, you would increase the proportion of direct sound from the speakers and hear the speaker the way the manufacturer intended, with little coloration from the room. This idea looked good on paper and on lab readouts, but fell short of perfection for the human beings using the rooms.

The first thing you would notice in these heavily padded spaces is that the audio perspective feels unnatural. If the room was well deadened, then it sucked all of the life out of every sound, including normal conversations. You could feel a cave-like audio vacuum all around you. Dead rooms literally absorb the audio power output from the speakers, and require you to crank them up more to get a satisfying level. Since then, we've learned that the best rooms for mixing have a combination of acoustic characteristics—not simply absorption—and have a satisfying "aliveness"—not just "deadness"—that makes them pleasant places in which to experience music. A well-conceived mixing room will not seriously affect the frequency response or some imaging of the speakers, yet it will have "life" and auditory spaciousness. Remember that starting off in a well-proportioned room with favorable dimensions is the best move you can make toward achieving an excellent listening environment.

Three Big Things to Remember

Sound waves traveling through the air are always affected when they make contact with objects and surfaces. They are affected by just three phenomena: *absorption, reflection,* and *diffusion.*

Absorption can be either partial or total; it occurs when sound waves encounter soft, porous, or flexible materials. The material dissipates the sound energy by turning it into heat energy (the amount of heat is almost immeasurable) instead of returning it back to the surrounding air. The way in which absorbent materials affect sound is dependent upon the frequency of the sound waves. In general, a soft, porous material (for instance, open-cell foam) is more absorbent at higher frequencies than at low frequencies. If the thickness of the material is increased, its ability to absorb low frequencies increases.

Reflection is the quality of bouncing sound waves back instead of trapping them. Where absorption is rarely total, reflection can be almost complete, and, not too surprisingly, unwanted reflection accounts for nearly all of the problems we try to correct in listening environments. High frequencies are reflected in specific directions, determined by the original direction from which they approach the surface. Low frequencies do not "follow directions," and when the size of the wave approaches the size of the reflecting surface, the wave is reflected strongly and omnidirectionally.

Diffusion is the ability of surfaces and objects to scatter incoming sound waves in multiple directions. Diffusion occurs when sound waves encounter "broken" or specially shaped surfaces. The important factor to remember about pure diffusion is that although sound is scattered in various directions, no sound energy is lost. In a diffusive surface, the larger and deeper the nooks, crannies, and variations, the lower the frequencies that will be affected. The most useful diffusers for room treatment are those that have many different-sized cavities and reflecting angles.

Go for the Big Problems First

One of the easiest approaches to room treatment is to go down to the store, buy some appropriate foamy-looking materials, slap them up on the walls in a suitably attractive manner, and feel like you've done your part to make the room look like it's supposed to be a mixing/listening environment. If you've kept up with this series so far, you know that this won't work. Cosmetic effects are not to be ignored, but the truth is that the way a room looks has almost nothing to do with how it performs sonically. Like doctors dealing with multiple injured patients in an emergency room, we need to look at the most serious problems first, and then deal with the lesser ones later, triage-style.

Almost every small- to mid-sized room has a problem with bass resonance, or standing waves. The remedy is something called a *bass trap*. There are several ways to approach bass trapping, and the size and shape of your room determines which one to use. Low-frequency waves tend to "build up," and they gain energy at the resonant frequencies of the room. The idea is to reduce the response of the room to these frequencies. There are three primary types of bass-trapping devices: resonant cavities, resonant panels, and soft absorbers. For small rooms, you can skip the resonant cavity idea because they are large and require significant construction; they're not something you can bring home from the store. Resonant panels are fairly large, thin, wood or masonite structures, specially mounted and tuned by carefully measured dimensions to vibrate with the offending bass frequencies, dissipating some of their energy. Usually, you must build these, although a couple of manufacturers sell ready-made units.

By far the most effective do-it-yourself bass-trapping approach is to use soft absorbers. It is now time to visualize your mixing environment and take a mental inventory of the objects currently in place. You may already have a soft bass absorber or two and not realize it. Bass absorption through soft materials has the greatest effect when the soft material has a large surface area, and when the material has adequate depth or thickness. Common objects that are good bass absorbers include plush, upholstered sofas—and if the sofa happens to contain a hide-a-bed with a mattress folded away inside, so much the better. In general, such a sofa in a listening room is a welcome addition, for practical reasons as well as sonic ones.

Walls and Corners

Low-frequency sound wave interaction in a room is concentrated where room boundaries intersect—in other words, in corners. That's where soft-absorber bass-trapping materials can be most effectively placed. The idea is to distribute the bass trapping around the room instead of putting it somewhere in one big lump. Bass trapping in the corners is sensible, because objects in corners won't tend to be in your way, and because corners contribute strongly to bass resonance problems.

A rectangular room has lots of corners, not just where the walls intersect, but also where walls meet floor and ceiling. It's better to avoid using up floor area with treatment materials, but the area of wall-to-ceiling intersections is a good place for acoustic materials, and three-way corners (two walls plus ceiling) are even better. Many of the commercially available bass-trapping devices and materials are designed for corner placement.

It is worthwhile to note that the performance of foam-based soft absorbers drops off as frequency decreases, and since independent testing labs' measurement criteria doesn't extend below 125 Hz, the makers don't claim any performance at all below that frequency. However, resonant panel absorbers can and do work below the cutoff testing frequency, down to below 40 Hz, and are available as modular units from several manufacturers.

Ordinary vs. Manufactured Acoustic Treatments

Home recordists have traditionally shown talents for improvisation with materials and techniques that would rival Martha Stewart ("Today we'll make a lovely microphone support out of nylon rope, clothespins, and an old inner tube..."). So using existing materials for acoustic room treatment comes naturally. A well-designed home recording/mixing environment often features a combination of ordinary objects and materials, along with specially manufactured acoustic materials. And always remember—every surface and object in a room affects acoustic response in some way.

In recent times, there has been a significant increase in the quality and variety of manufactured acoustic materials available for purchase by individuals. For years, only architects and acoustic designers were aware of such products, but now the whole gamut of absorbers, diffusers, and other materials can be purchased at large music and audio-visual dealers, as well as directly from manufacturers via mail-order. The greatest advantage of using manufactured acoustic treatments is that you know you are getting products of known and measured performance.

But there is much to recommend regarding the use of everyday materials in the studio. For one thing, they look like they belong and, whereas manufactured acoustic materials look high-tech and industrial, common objects and materials can create a homey, residential feel. In fact, some commercial studios located in industrial buildings use residential-looking materials to create a comfy ambience while still controlling audio characteristics. In most cases, the common materials cost less, and sometimes it's just a matter of taking things you already have and using them for their acoustical properties. A plush sofa bed becomes a bass absorber, a bookshelf unit with randomly sized books pinch-hits as a diffuser, and a quilted wall hanging is a flat-panel absorber to suck up flutter echoes. Carpeting, either partial or wall-to-wall, makes an immediate impact in rooms that are too reflective at mid and high frequencies.

What you can't do with everyday objects is predict exact results; you end up experimenting with parameters you can't measure. The best you can do is understand what the various materials and objects do in general, figure out what the room needs most, introduce the objects and materials, and see what happens. It requires careful listening, but one advantage is that you probably already have some of the objects, and it's just a matter of moving them in and out of the room in the name of experimentation.

A recent development of interest to all home and project-studio recordists is the availability of pre-designed acoustic treatment kits now offered by several suppliers. These "studio-in-a-box" concepts feature a coordinated collection of bass trapping, distributed absorption, and diffusion materials with step-by-step instructions on how and where to install them. The designers of these kits worked from the idea that many typical rooms you'd want to use for monitoring have similar characteristics and problems. For $300 to $500 per kit, these systems are a great idea for recordists who don't want to experiment and need to achieve quick acoustic results. As advertised, they will yield a useful acoustic improvement for the most common room problems. However, your mileage may vary, as they say, and these kits might be more or less than what your room needs. Always use your common sense when considering all-in-one solutions.

Acoustic Foam Is King

As you scan the catalogs and websites of acoustic treatment manufacturers, you quickly discover that many of the items offered are made of *acoustic foam*. It is a material extremely well suited for controlling room acoustics. Not just any generic foam will work, because there are many different types of plastic and rubber foam used for everything from sealing the doors in your car to padding the insides of shipping cartons. Acoustic foam has specific characteristics including a special internal open-cell structure, controlled density (it is much heavier than some other foams), the ability to resist environmental contaminants in the air (carbon dioxide, smoke, and UV) without deteriorating, and flame retardant ratings. In addition, suppliers offer different acoustic foams with characteristics specially tailored for controlling specific frequency ranges.

The most important characteristic of acoustic foam is that it has been tested and measured to produce a specific result when used according to the maker's recommendations. You pay more than you would for generic materials (although many acoustic foam products are reasonably priced and represent great value), but you get the benefit of research and testing.

Diffusers

One of the most interesting acoustic developments of the last few years is the use of manufactured diffuser units for home/project studios and control rooms. Diffusers scatter the incoming sound waves in a way that is nearly omnidirectional, giving an open, airy feel, and without draining away acoustic energy. The key to the effective use of diffusers is positioning.

Quality monitors have good high-frequency dispersion—mids and highs are spread out in a hemisphere shape instead of being beamed straight forward. Though the speakers are pointed at the listener, more or less, high frequencies fan out well to the sides. To control what are called *first reflections* from the monitors, manufacturers recommend placing diffuser units on the side walls in front of the speaker position. A typical diffuser is an 8'x8' square, or two 2'x2' square units. You can also kill first reflections using foam absorbers—say four or six 12"x12" units on each side, but spaced apart so that there is a bit of hard wall surface exposed (about 3" or 4") between the units. This arrangement simulates the effect of diffusers but with the added absorption of highs—just the opposite effect of a diffuser. The goal in either case is to tame first reflections.

Along with the side wall diffuser locations, another useful spot is the center of the rear wall of the control room. The desired effects here are spaciousness and freedom from the slap echo that can originate from that spot if it's not covered with absorbent materials.

Leaving Soon?

To many recordists, the terms "acoustic treatment" and "rental space" are mutually exclusive. Just when you are ready to order the instant studio treatment kit, you notice that it includes large tubes of special mounting adhesive. Before you start having visions of your rental deposit fluttering into the waste can because you've defaced the walls, you should realize that the acoustic treatment world has ways of working with leased space.

For starters, you can drive a few nails in the wall—as long as they aren't huge spikes and you remember to remove them and patch up the holes before moving day. One of the ways to mount foam panels, especially thick ones, is to drive a few headless finish nails partially into the wall, leaving them about halfway exposed, and then hang the foam object directly on them, with the head end of the nail poking into the foam. This method won't work for thin sheets of foam, as they tend to droop when held just in a few places.

Some acoustic foam manufacturers have designed systems of backing panel and Velcro® tabs to secure their products semipermanently. Rest assured that the material suppliers have faced numerous obstacles in both commercial and residential installations, and here again you can benefit from years of experience when you use their recommended mounting methods and systems.

There have also been significant developments in the last few years in portable acoustic treatment devices. They create new ways to use your workspace for multiple purposes—one of which is playback monitoring and mixing, and another is the creation of temporary monitoring environments for on-location recording. Most of these portable devices are fairly lightweight, self-contained, and require very little setup time. Since the usual goal is to correct overly abundant reflectivity and runaway bass resonance, the portable devices are usually constructed of good old reliable acoustic foam. One manufacturer, Auralex Acoustics, even offers a whole system of free-standing foam wall units that can be used to construct a room-within-a-room on a temporary or semipermanent basis.

Looks Count

Here's a dirty little acoustic secret that I wish I could have exploited as a kid to explain the condition of neglect in my bedroom: Random junk is good, acoustically speaking. I have a room where I work occasionally with a collection of guitar cases and equipment containers stacked high along the rear wall. Though there isn't a lot of official acoustic treatment beyond a good area rug over a wood floor and mini-blinds on the windows, the room sounds well controlled, with a pleasing character and almost no annoying flutter echo. The mass of "stuff" is providing significant broadband diffusion.

If looks don't matter, you can get away with using the "clutter factor" as part of your acoustic design. But many people prefer orderliness in workspaces, and if you are bringing in players and clients, having a neat, professional-looking studio space does matter. If you choose to go heavy on manufactured absorption and diffusion units, the room will have a definite industrial/tech look, which many people feel to be part of the studio vibe. You can, however, achieve a pleasing combination of traditional furnishings along with specialty materials that will be acoustically effective yet will feel "at home" and harmonious with everyday living.

Go Forth Now—Absorb, Diffuse, and Reflect . . .

We've covered a lot of ground in this series: speaker choices, room layout, and treatment strategies. The goal is to have a comfortable monitoring environment that you can occupy for hours at a stretch, and in which you can make good mixing decisions that will play well on other listening systems. Most studios—especially home studios—are in a constant state of flux and refinement. Continual refinement of the acoustic character of your rooms is part of the challenge—and part of the great fun—of home recording.

Ten Guidelines for Acoustic Room Treatment

1. There are only three phenomena that affect sound waves in an enclosed space: absorption, diffusion, and reflection. A good monitoring environment will take advantage of all three.

2. Most rooms come equipped with—at no extra charge—an abundance of sound reflectivity. Room treatments seek to reduce the proportion of reflectivity by adding diffusion and absorption.

3. Some rooms are "harder" than others. A room with concrete walls and floor (e.g., a basement) has much higher reflectivity at all frequencies than a room with gypsum wallboard over wood studs and a wood floor. These materials actually flex slightly in response to sound and dissipate bass energy, whereas concrete rooms require serious absorption in most cases.

4. Most rooms can benefit from bass trapping—the absorption of low-frequency energy at 200 Hz and below. Thick, soft, porous materials may be used as bass absorbers. Soft bass-absorption materials may be distributed throughout a room, and work best at the front of a room (i.e., the speaker end) and in corners.

5. Absorption depletes overall energy from sound sources. Diffusion maintains overall energy.

6. Many absorbent devices and materials are made of acoustic foam. In general, as foam gets thicker, its absorption at lower frequencies increases. Thin foam (1/2" thickness) has almost no effect on bass frequencies. Typical foam bass absorbers are very thick—at least 6" to 12".

7. Sound-absorbing materials offer greater benefit if they are distributed around a room instead of all being placed in one area. Contrary to what you may have seen in studio and control room photographs, wall-to-wall overall absorbent covering is not required or desirable for controlling the acoustics in typical mixdown rooms.

8. Always consider using common materials for room treatment—upholstered furniture, vertical-slat blinds, draperies, wall hangings, and carpet—when possible. They not only achieve acoustic objectives, but also have practical and aesthetic benefits.

9. Be aware that large, flat equipment surfaces and gear racks contribute reflectivity where it is least desired. Try to place them so that they will not disturb the acoustic profile of the room or serve as sources of unwanted reflections.

10. If you have the luxury of choosing among several rooms for your monitoring environment, try to choose one with non-integral proportions (i.e., a room whose dimensions are not divisible by the same whole number). For example, a room that's 12'x12'x3' (all dimensions evenly divisible by four) will be much harder to tame than a room that's 10'x14'x8', even though both rooms have about the same amount space.

Recording

Ch-Ch-Ch-Ch-Changes
Technology Marches On
By David Darlington

Not long ago, musicians lusted after expensive synths, samplers, and drum machines just to create a basic demo. Often, the price tags allowed the average working musician only one or two high-end pieces of gear in their arsenal. Today, samplers are contained on less expensive PCI cards or run on a computer's native CPU, further lowering the cost. Entire sample libraries can be stored on a big, cheap FireWire drive instead of a confusing array of floppy disks, CD-ROMs, or removable cartridges. Sample collections can be organized as drag-and-drop computer files so that they're easy to find and collate, and the samplers themselves operate from within the sequencing software. In addition to samplers, many third-party developers offer synth engines that run on your desktop and interface smoothly with your favorite sequencer. Today, a single computer can be a drum machine, a loop player, and a multichannel synth all at once; the sounds as well as the performances can be quantized, shifted, transposed, and otherwise edited in real time. Talk about your band-in-a-box!

To make an album ten years ago, the average band recorded on 2" analog tape, which cost about $200 per roll and held about three songs per roll. If you required more than 24 tracks, you needed two tapes (48 tracks), thereby doubling your tape costs. Later, digital tape became common, but it was also very expensive; on top of this, there was the cost of going into a studio that was big enough to afford the original large-format digital tape machines. Personal multitracks were available, but they couldn't offer big-studio quality. All of that changed with the advent of modular digital multitracks (MDMs) like the TASCAM DA-88 and Alesis ADAT formats. Suddenly, high-quality digital recording was inexpensive. The reign of these ice-age beasts was short, however. Since digital recording consists of number crunching, and powerful desktop computers can crunch with the best of them, the recording platforms of choice soon became Macs and PCs.

Need a bunch of outboard gear to mix your CD? Years ago, it was helpful to have a banker in your family in order to afford enough gear to make an acceptable mix. Automated consoles were beyond the reach of all but the most credit-worthy corporations, and individual signal processors cost thousands of dollars each. Now, small-footprint consoles feature automation that their predecessors only dreamed of, and desktop digital audio workstations provide even more powerful automation. Plug-ins offer every type of sound manipulation known to humankind, and a single plug-in can be applied

106

to many individual channels at once, thus saving space and money. Presets can be saved, mixes stored, and entire studio setups recalled with mere button pushes.

Probably one of the most dramatic changes in recent years has been in the amount of space required to make music. Since many sounds now originate on the desktop, and most of the work is being done on small footprint consoles, studios themselves have shrunk dramatically in the last few years. Of course, if you need to cut a live band, you still need a large live space, but many great records are currently being created in modest control rooms with just enough space for proper monitoring. Single overdubs with the likes of vocals, horns, or guitar don't require a lot of room; a small isolation booth works fine. So now, even a small room in a private home can become a decent facility.

Unconventional Wisdom
Exploding the 12 Great Myths About Recording
By Pat Kirtley

Myths are fun to read about. We are fascinated by the stories of the heroic adventures of Hercules, Odysseus, Thor, and Atlas. We even love them—but we don't believe them. They are the work of great writers with bizarre, fertile imaginations and wonderful story lines. And they always illustrate some very real aspect of the human predicament.

The myths of the audio and recording world can be fun, too, as long as we take the time to sort out truth from fiction. Audio myths take root in several ways. Nostalgia—the notion that older is better—gives us the vintage microphone syndrome and tube envy. Wishful thinking has us wanting to believe that we can do studio-quality mastering with a $79 PC sound card and turn our recordings into instant masterpieces with something called an "enhancer." Paranoia keeps us obsessing about whether analog really is better than digital and gets us scared about the horrific bed of digital crud always lurking just beyond our naive perception. And blind faith raises our confidence in the existence of some desktop audio wonderland, where twisting a little virtual knob on a screen can magically remove all noise and emulate thousands of dollars' worth of high-end outboard equipment.

So let's examine some compelling stories from the audio world, blow apart the ones that don't make any sense, and dig back into the twisted history to uncover the ever-present seedlings of truth from which germinate the wildest tales.

Myth 1: Tubes Good, Solid-State Bad (with Apologies to Dr. Frankenstein's Monster)

This one started out in the late 1950s when the first transistor-based audio amplifiers were offered to audiophiles. They held the promise of smaller size, robust dependability, and less heat, but the audio performance of the first couple of generations of amplifiers left a lot to be desired. Notably, the kind of distortion produced by the early solid-state designs when accidentally overdriven was very unpleasant to the ear, and the original transistor types had noticeably higher noise and distortion even at soft levels. The very idea that transistors with such bad performance could ever replace tubes was laughable to audio know-it-alls.

The same thing happened all over again in the musician's world in the early '60s when the first solid-state guitar and keyboard amps were introduced. Here, the backlash was worse because musicians were beginning to utilize overdriven tube amplifiers to get desirable new tones. The early solid-state designs sounded edgy (in a *bad* way) when accidentally overdriven, but downright awful when this was done intentionally. The engineers went back to the drawing boards, eventually producing exquisite, reliable, solid-state designs, but somehow the stigma remained, and repercussions still echo today.

Here's the bottom line on this topic: The world now runs on solid-state audio equipment. It is virtually impossible to create a recording of any kind without going through numerous stages of solid-state electronics. The excellent results possible are obvious every time you turn on your CD player. What are tubes good for? Well, they can't be beat when you want to get a fat overdriven sound from an instrument, and high-end microphones with onboard tube impedance converters are great. The pleasant overload characteristics of tube-based mic preamps can be worth their prices. Beyond that, tube equipment has a warm nostalgic glow that is especially pleasing (with a nice mug of hot cider) in northern winters.

Myth 2: Hotter Levels Are Better

The quest for perceived loudness began in the days when AM radio was an important force in the music world. In the early days, there were usually only one or two stations serving a broadcast area. But by the 1950s, some metropolitan areas became saturated with stations, all close by and capable of providing a strong signal to thousands of receivers. Engineers discovered that they could make a station pop out from its neighbors on the dial by maximizing the average audio level to the transmitter. Since the FCC strictly limited modulation peaks to 100 percent or less (by law, you couldn't distort the audio at the transmitter), engineers learned to use a slick new device called a compressor to raise the average level without going over the FCC mark. "Hotter is better" became the buzz phrase in 1950s AM broadcasting, and the idea was still in full flower when the 1960s FM giants were marketing album-oriented rock.

The concept carried over to the recording studio, where some engineers intentionally saturated the tape by recording some sounds (typically vocals, bass, and drums) way over zero on the meters. The results, when successful, yielded a fat, squashed sound that was not at all unpleasant in a mix. Engineers further squished the dynamics in the final mix, employing the same logic as used in AM radio, but here, instead of making a station stand out on the dial, the technique could make your hopeful hit single "pop out" when played in succession with others on a jukebox.

So much for the successful loudness strategies of the rock era. Today, with digital-based equipment prevailing, trying to get a hotter sound by kicking things up against the meter's limits won't get you anywhere. What the 0 dB metering point on digital recorders represents is kind of an audio brick wall, beyond which no further levels can be tolerated. If you violate digital zero by just a few decibels, the resultant clipping—rather than the addition of a fat analog punchiness—sounds curiously like the crud that sent the 1950s transistor-amp haters running into the streets.

The key is to record untamed first-generation material by carefully maintaining an adequate cushion of a few decibels near the top of the digital meters. At the same time, beware of setting the levels too low, which causes a loss of bit depth and hurts the quality of sounds on the quiet end of the loudness spectrum. Then, at mixdown time, perceived loudness or *peak-to-average level proportion* can be tweaked by the judicious use of devices or programs designed for the purpose. If a hot, stressed sound is desired, you are now back to using compression and limiting like the AM radio engineers did in the late 1950s—and no cheating with recorders.

Open-minded recordists can be freed from the tyranny of "hotter is better" and begin thinking of dynamic range as one of the sound qualities—like EQ and ambience—that can be sculpted in a number of ways to get a desired result.

Myth 3: Analog Is Better Than Digital

This myth took root in the early days of digital audio recording, around 1980. The precision A/D and D/A converters we have today were just a dream then, but analog tape recorders had reached a high state of perfection. These machines also represented a hefty investment for studio owners, and this investment needed to be preserved. Even if digital was better and would become the standard method of recording, studios couldn't dump perfectly functioning current machinery in favor of it. So, there was a lot of head-shaking and nay-saying at the time. The lack of audio perfection in the first CD players (and CDs themselves) dampened the spirits of audio purists, too, so digital had an all-around bad rap to overcome.

All of that is now in the past. The truth is that most audio now goes through digital stages in the recording process, and it's often distributed to the listener by digital means. Digital is the state of the art in all recording, both audio and video. In practical terms, this technology has cured more ills than it has created, and if you want to talk about it in terms of battlefields and warriors, digital has claimed the higher ground.

Myth 4: Digital Is Better Than Analog

Analog technology, in the realm of recording, reached a significant state of perfection. The best analog recording equipment is unquestionably good enough for the demands of any musical requirement. In fact, analog systems have been the yardstick for the development of digital technology. In terms of quality, the best digital systems are essentially equal to the best of analog.

What's implied by this myth is that analog is now deserving of the dust heap, but that's a shortsighted conclusion. Especially for home recordists, there is a gold mine of quite serviceable open-reel analog multitrack recorders to be found on the used market, from manufacturers like TEAC, TASCAM, and Fostex. You can buy this equipment for a song, learn to use it well, and have the last laugh as everyone else struggles to cope with the wrinkles of digital multitracking. Compared to some of the cheap and inadequate digital solutions being offered, quality analog machines often do indeed have warmer and sweeter sounds. Just remember to keep those tape heads clean!

Myth 5: Digital Is Digital

When people say this, they are implying that once audio is in digital form, it's great, awesome, perfect, and impervious to any assault. It's a reassuring thought, but dangerous to take at face value. The problem is that there is a lot of cheaply designed and produced digital technology lurking out there, especially in the desktop computer arena, offering more in the way of marketing hype than in performance.

You can avoid getting caught up in this nightmare of substandards by trusting your ears and using common sense. You aren't going to buy a state-of-the-art digital sound card for your computer for $79, even though the wording on the package insists that you are getting "CD quality." A realistic approach is to research the market, find out what the pros are using, and see if it's reasonable for you to afford and benefit from it. Don't expect something for nothing, especially if it's already "free"—and also includes a "game accelerator" feature. It's best to pass off "digital is digital" as just the empty phrase that it is—there is no quick, dirty, or automatic way to achieve true, lasting quality.

Myth 6: You Can Fix It in the Mix

This myth is as old as the punch-in/punch-out multitrack recording technology that first surfaced in the late 1960s. It's as old as mixing itself, and it is largely wishful thinking. In the world of design and engineering, it is a well-known fact that quality comes more from planning and ground-up thinking than from last-minute fixes or final cosmetic changes. This is also true in the music production world.

You should strive for quality at every stage of every project. Once I submitted some demo tracks to a major record producer for a new project, and they were passed over (or ignored—you can't tell the difference). I knew that the music was exactly what they were looking for, but I had been in a hurry and went for the dangerous "quick demo tape." I was out of town for a week, so on the road I borrowed a friend's pocket mini-disc recorder and an inexpensive Sony stereo mic and made the recordings in a living room. When I brought the DAT transfer back home and dumped it to my computer workstation, I realized that it didn't sound too great, but I fell under the tempting notion that I could fix it anyway, what with all of the knobs and gizmos at my disposal. Upon listening to this little project a few months later, I could understand why the music wasn't chosen. The performance was fine, but the tone quality sounded like it was coming from an empty coffee can via a tightly stretched piece of string. That's a bit of an exaggeration, but I had bought into the fix-it-in-the-mix myth and paid the price. Remember: Demo means *demonstration*—in other words, a demonstration of how good you do what you do—but it's never an excuse for substandard audio or production.

There are quite a few things you can fix in the mix. Tonal balance and levels between instruments and voices are what the art of mixing is all about. But the mix is never a place to try to regain the overall audio integrity that was somehow lost at a previous stage.

Myth 7: I Can Make My Own CD Master!

This one is really scary. It wasn't long ago that the CD mastering process involved literally hundreds of thousands of dollars' worth of esoteric equipment in the hands of laboratory experts. It really isn't surprising that people who think that they can simply purchase a few hundred dollars' worth of gadgets and whip out CD masters end up disappointed and frustrated. There is far more to this process than meets the eye.

The technical requirements for the coding that goes onto the surface of a CD (length codes, table of contents, and countdowns) are far from trivial. Mastering is not just a "nice touch"—it's a requirement. Most musicians and self-recordists who are otherwise capable of making decent recordings of their music don't have a clue about what goes on in the digital stream beneath the surface of that polycarbonate and aluminum disc. You could take the time to learn all about it, but this is one of those areas where the benefits of a lifetime of skill and judgment can be rented at reasonable rates in the form of the services of a mastering engineer. Beyond the application of a second set of experienced ears to your project, a mastering engineer can ensure that the resulting master CD will comply with all specifications—which ensures that it can be replicated without a fuss and every copy will be playable in virtually every CD player. It doesn't even cost much, so don't fall into this easily avoided trap.

Myth 8: Noise Introduced at an Early Recording Stage Can Be Removed Later

It can't. Freedom from electronically produced noise (hiss, hum, and crackles) is one of the reasons you should use the best equipment available to you at all stages of a project. Yes, there are noise elimination and reduction devices that claim to remove such artifacts when they occur, and sometimes these processes are moderately successful. But the truth here is that one dollar spent to buy better equipment (e.g., microphones and preamps) for the early stage of the recording process is easily worth ten dollars in sound repair at the final stages. Near perfection (in terms of freedom from noise and distortion) is probably within your reach when it comes to basic recording equipment, so don't scrimp on *any* component in the signal path.

Myth 9: You Can "Do It All" on a PC with a Digital Recording Card and Software

A virtual recording studio in a box! Cheap desktop computer-based audio workstations will dominate recording and put the studios out of business!

I first heard this over seven years ago. It wasn't logical then and it still isn't now (see below).

Myth 9a: I Don't Need Any Outboard Gear Because My Desktop Computer Can Create Every Known Effect with Software

This is probably the newest myth of the bunch, because the idea that outboard gear can be simulated by software and DSP (digital signal processing) chips is a relatively recent one. This technology, which holds great promise, simply isn't ready for primetime yet— at least not on your typical personal computer. There are instances where some aspects of it do function as advertised, but it's expensive, requiring state-of-the-art computing systems with high-end digital audio engines installed.

There are lots of software titles out there for audio that appear to have every processing tool known to mankind, from reverb to micro-band EQ to time compression— some of them selling for way under $100. If you are fooled by the unbelievably low prices, your ears won't be fooled by the unbelievably bad results that most of these cheap solutions offer. It's easy for a software designer to make it look like the software has a particular function, but it's way harder to make that function work as promised.

I had a frustrating discussion recently with a video edit engineer who told me that we didn't need to utilize the stereo audio tracks on a video production we were doing because his digital audio software could "turn anything into stereo." And, by golly, there was a little button on his computer screen labeled "stereoize." Some people will believe anything.

Real outboard gear is here to stay for a while.

Myth 10: "Enhancers" Can Make Amateur Recordings Sound Like Those Made by the Pros

I've always been afraid of audio machines whose marketers are reluctant (or unable) to tell me exactly what they do. Talk about your magic bullets—the people who market "enhancers" generate more double-talk than politicians. "What does your product do?" "Well, it just makes everything sound better!" "How does it do that?" "Well, our proprietary redactile perusification technology allows blah, blah, blah . . ."

The thought that always comes to my mind when I think of these magic boxes is that if the enhancement is so pleasing and so automatic, then why don't Sony, RCA, Panasonic, and everyone else simply include the circuitry in every TV, stereo, computer, and boom box they manufacture? You know, kind of like the "spatial-X" and "Sensory-3D" stuff that they often throw in already (and that most people seem to never use). Then, if you could produce your recordings with an aural enhancer, and the listener's boom box could enhance it even more, wouldn't that be great?

It probably wouldn't. In professional video equipment, for instance, there are internal controls to regulate horizontal and vertical picture enhancement—an increase in sharpness beyond what is actually present in the signal. Video engineers learn early on that there is a correct setting for these controls, and going beyond that point (too much enhancement) results in a picture that looks very "sharp" but noisy and artificial. What audio enhancers can do is add a little oomph and sparkle to the sound—a finishing touch, if you will. But I've never heard of anyone using these devices to turn a mediocre recording into a professional master.

Myth 11: Great Recordings Are Made with Cheap Monitor Speakers

In every big-business, hit-making recording factory you can find at least one pair of cheap monitors. They usually are perched right on top of the console, and the engineers and producers can switch over and listen to them at any time instead of the megabuck Goliaths mounted in the wall. Since these little boxes are so visible, it's easy to think that this is how the hits are made and, with a little wishful thinking, that you can get away with using these little guys as your only monitors. In the recording business, these speakers are known as the *bad reference*—a necessary evil that tells you whether your mix is going to play alright on all of the dock radios and TV speakers of the world where, admittedly, a lot of consumer listening is done. The little speakers are always used in addition to the real monitors, just to see if everything will still be there on a severely compromised playback system.

Real monitors are specialty speakers that feature wide frequency response so that you hear all of what's in the mix (even the problematic bad stuff), rugged power handling to tolerate all-day usage, low distortion so the engineers' and producers' ears don't get worn out quickly, and a lack of coloration so that the attractiveness of the sound comes from what is in the recording instead of what the speakers create. These monitors tend to be expensive, but the good ones are worth every penny.

Myth 12: Louder Is Better

Of course it is!

Pre-Production
The Session Before the Session
By Rusty Cutchin

One of the great advantages of a home studio is the freedom to work at your own pace without the constraints and pressures of working in a commercial facility. At some point, however, you will want to take your projects to an outside studio for various reasons. When that time comes, the critical first step is to look carefully at everything you can accomplish in pre-production—before the clock starts and the costs mount up.

Often, the smallest things can break the back of a recording session and ruin the day of everyone involved. Recently, I was at a demo session for a young band and the musicians were understandably excited about getting their songs on tape. The drummer carefully set up his kit and began to warm up with some ferocious beats and fills that got everyone in the room pumped. The guitar player went through several settings on his Marshall stack until he had the "tone of doom" neatly corralled and ready to let loose. And the bass player was slamming his strings like a jackhammer operator at an industrial dig.

The engineer had the band miked perfectly, the entourage had the appropriate adoring gazes, the drummer clicked the count, and off they went. The first couple of takes went smoothly, with the vocalist making minor adjustments to lyrics and arguing briefly with the guitar player about the length of the intro. They had just kicked off the third take when the bass player snapped his low E string like a twig in a hurricane.

Everyone in the band just looked at each other as if to say, "Wow, man, that never happened before."

So, this is a minor interruption, right? The bass player changes his string and the session resumes? Nope—the bass player had no extra strings. Could the bass player perhaps play some notes up an octave so the drums and guitar could be recorded and the final bass overdubbed later? Nope—the bass player wasn't skillful enough on the instrument to do that. The session was on a weeknight so there was no chance of buying strings. Session over. Everybody went home. The band was disappointed, the engineer lost his night's pay, and the project was postponed.

These kinds of problems crop up all of the time, but it's easy to avoid them and keep a session on track if you keep a little checklist of things you need to prepare for and accomplish before going into a studio. Here's a list of things to take into consideration so your recording session won't get derailed.

Rehearsal

This is the only kind of pre-production there used to be. Especially for bands, fine-tuning and working the kinks out of songs that have to be performed together makes for a smoother, tension-free session when everyone is watching the clock. Even if costs are not a factor, there is less fatigue and more enthusiasm when a band can play their tunes with authority and concentrate on the details rather than chord changes and lyrics.

Computer Literacy

If you're taking sequences or samples into someone else's studio, bring backups. Whatever media you're using to store your project—portable hard drive, CD-RW, Zip disc, etc.—is fragile. It will fail at some point—maybe at your session. Never assume that files on a CD-R will load into the studio's computer flawlessly, or that the studio's computer has the same programs and extensions as the system on which the tunes were programmed. Contact the studio and see what their setup is, prepare accordingly, and *always bring backups*.

Communication

Talk as often as you need to with the studio owner or engineer about their capabilities, what equipment you're bringing, and what issues might come up about interfacing your equipment with the studio's. If you're paying for a big commercial room, make sure that you understand what constitutes "down time" and what doesn't. Remember that the studio won't be concerned about your lack of preparedness, especially if you're paying an hourly rate.

Be Realistic

Set reasonable limits on what can be accomplished in a given time frame. High energy and enthusiasm will make you want to do the whole project in one night, but fatigue can impair judgment and destroy the ability to judge a mix critically.

Think Carefully About the "Crew"

Sure, everybody wants their buddies and their girlfriends around them when they're recording, but the distractions, input, noise, and confusion of the entourage almost always slows down and complicates the session. It also inhibits communication between the artist and producer or engineer who must work together to get the artist's concepts faithfully on tape.

Murphy (Not Clapton) Rules

Therefore, assume that everything that can go wrong will go wrong in the studio and bring at least two of everything: lyric sheets, picks, checks (you didn't forget about paying, did you?), and—oh yeah—bass strings.

Isolation on the Cheap

By Mike Levine

If your recording projects feature vocals as well as other instruments that must be miked, having a recording space that is isolated from your control room can greatly enhance your ability to cut good, clear tracks. And while you might think that isolation booths and live rooms are strictly for big-time studios, you can, in fact, utilize an existing room in your house as an isolated recording space for about the same amount of money as it would cost to buy a pizza, a six-pack of beer, and a couple of tickets to the movies.

But first, let's look at why you need isolation when recording. Having the talent record in an acoustically separate space has a number of advantages. First, you (the engineer) are freed from wearing headphones and can listen to the signals coming in from the mics directly through your studio monitors. This makes it much easier to evaluate the "sound" you're getting and make better decisions regarding mic placement, compression, and EQ. Having a separate live room also eliminates the problem of gear and computer noise leaking through the mics onto the tracks.

So how do you do it? The trick is to extend your mic and headphone cables so that they reach another room in your house that is (at least somewhat) acoustically isolated from your main studio. Any room—even a hallway—can do the trick. Since you probably won't be able to dedicate this second room as a full-time adjunct to your studio, you'll be pleased to know that it's very easy to set up and break down your own iso room—in fact, it takes only minutes. It's probably best to choose a room that's carpeted and doesn't get a lot of outside noise (e.g., don't use the room overlooking the dog kennel).

In order to set up your iso room, you'll need to get one or more headphone extension cables. Measure the distance between the headphone out in your control room and the iso room and add about 8' (for slack)—that's how much headphone extension cable you'll need. If one extension cable isn't long enough, you can buy two and use the second to extend the first. You should also buy one or two headphone splitter jacks so you can plug in more than one set of cans in your iso room. (If you're going to be doing this often, you should also consider buying a headphone amp.) Run the cable under your studio door and along the floor until it reaches the iso room.

Although you could plug this extension cable into the headphone jack on your mixer, you're better off using the headphone jack on a DAT or other piece of recording gear that's plugged into the master (LR) out of your mixer. The reason for this is that the mix passing through the mixer's headphone jack is affected when you solo a channel, which can cause major problems for the singer or instrumentalist who is being recorded. The mix coming out of the master out, however, is unaffected when you solo a channel. You can also route your headphone mix through an aux send on your mixer and connect the corresponding aux output to your DAT or recording gear.

You'll also most probably need to buy additional (or longer) mic cables in order to cover the distance from your mixer or mic pre to your iso room. The other issue that needs to be addressed is talkback. You'll be able to hear your talent talking to you through the mic (or mics) that you're recording them with, but they also need to hear you for instructions and comments. Unfortunately, if you're deriving your headphone mix from a DAT machine or other two-track that's connected to the master outs of your mixer, then the talkback mic (if you have one) on your mixer will not be audible to those listening on headphones. You'll need to plug a mic into your mixer and send it to the master outputs. Just don't bus it to the multitrack channel(s) you're recording on, or the signal from it could end up on tape or disk.

Obviously, building a permanent booth should be your ultimate goal, but until your studio is busy enough to justify that expense, this temporary, inexpensive setup can make your recording life a whole lot easier.

Vocals 101
Tips for Getting the Best from Your Singer
By David Darlington

So, your beats are banging, the chords are off the hook, and you finally wrote down that classic chorus melody that's been in your head. Now it's time to record the vocalist and put the finishing touch on the masterpiece. People ask me all of the time if there is a secret for cutting a great vocal. Well, there isn't exactly a secret, but there are a few things to consider before the session.

The first, of course, is the microphone. Affordable mics fall into two general categories: *dynamic* and *condenser*. Dynamic mics are usually less expensive and can withstand higher sound pressure levels. This makes them great for screaming rock or blazing, hip-hop vocalists who tend to be on full blast all the time.

Dynamic mics have the added advantage of rejecting sound that isn't directly in front of the mic. This is good if, as in many home studios, the acoustic environment leaves something to be desired (Was that an ambulance or did the guitarist come in too early?). The singer can actually be in the control room if you keep the overall volume at a manageable level (there is a famous artist in New York City who recorded all of his hits from the control room couch this way). Dynamic mics are often used in pro studios, and good ones are available for a few hundred bucks or less. The most common ones are the Shure SM57 and SM58, the Sennheiser MD421, and a number of models by Beyer.

If your budget allows, a condenser mic offers a wider dynamic range and generally picks up more subtleties in the sound. These mics have larger capsules and require electric power, usually a +48v signal that is provided by your console or mic preamp via a wire on the microphone cable. This is what is known as *phantom power*. Usually there is a switch that engages phantom power on the mixer or preamp in order for the mic to work.

Condenser mics are warm and clear and are used all over the world for vocals. Some of the more popular models are the AKG 414, the Neumann U87, and the Audio-Technica 4000 series. If you choose this kind of mic for your vocalist, you'll need a "pop" filter to keep explosive consonants from distorting the capsule. Inexpensive pop screens are available at music stores. Put the screen directly in front of the capsule and about 1.5" to 2" away from it. Try to position it unobtrusively so that it doesn't obstruct your view of, or hinder your communication with, the vocalist. Make sure that the singer can still see the lyrics, if necessary.

A mic preamp can have a big effect on the sound quality. Solid-state mic pre's are considered cleaner sounding, and tube-based mic pre's are considered warmer. If you are tracking to a digital-format recorder, you will benefit from a tube circuit to give body and warmth to your vocal sound. These mic pre's are also great for recording guitars, synths, and drums.

In general, you'll find that the channels on most consoles do not have great mic pre's unless you're working with high-quality pro-level boards such as those from Neve or API. This is because manufacturers need to keep costs down. However, if you're recording only one or two inputs at a time, you may be able to invest in a high-quality outboard preamp.

The environment has everything to do with the immediacy of a vocal sound. Don't record in a roomy space like a garage, a bathroom, or a stairwell unless you really have to or you want an altered sound. Once the natural ambience of a poor-sounding room is recorded, it's almost impossible to remove it with EQ or processing. It's much better to record vocals in a dry, dead space and then add reverb and delay later. Use a walk-in closet, or drape blankets around the space where the singer will be to deaden any reflections. Make the space quiet so that the vocal will be "in your face."

Also, consider the vocalist's comfort. A comfortable singer is a happy (and, often, more in-tune) singer. Make sure that there is good light, or mood light if required, and make sure that the room temperature is comfortable. Singers tend to hate air conditioning because the cold air tightens their throats, so cool that room down before the session and then turn off the AC.

Finally, make sure that the singer can hear well so that he or she can sing comfortably. Taking an extra minute or two with the headphone mix can save you hours of retakes and avoid singer fatigue. Try grouping the music separately from the voice so that you can easily control each of their relative volumes. That way, when the vocalist says "I can't hear myself" you can bring down the track and bring up the overall level without losing the music mix. Invest in a decent pair of headphones—preferably ones with enclosed earcups, not open foam. This will keep leakage to a minimum. Don't listen too loudly when tracking in a non-isolated space or the speakers might leak into your vocal track.

Making the singer (and yourself) comfortable is the best thing you can do to ensure a great take and successful session. Now, all you need is a hit song!

Singers Unlimited
Techniques for Vocal Comping
By David Darlington

Sometimes a final lead vocal track is the result of not only a great singer's performance but also a clever engineer's editing abilities. Even the best vocalists seldom get a final version in one take, so the engineer's job is to create one flawless performance from a number of consistently good ones. The final *comp* (composite track) must be seamless, transparent, and natural in a way that maintains the electricity created by the music.

Before the singer arrives, create several new vocal tracks in your software and assign them to the proper inputs and outputs. This will speed the recording of multiple vocal takes by enabling you to mute and arm new tracks without having to make adjustments to the mix. Assign all of the vocal tracks the same delay or reverb so the sound remains consistent from take to take. Familiarize yourself with the form of the song as soon as you can and create markers, or *locate points*, so you can jump to any section rapidly.

The individual vocal tracks must stay consistent in level, tone, and compression, and getting the sound right up front will save you headaches later. As the singer warms up and gains confidence, you will probably need to make subtle reductions in level and compression to keep a uniform quality from track to track. It's easy to monitor levels on a digital audio workstation, and you can visually note the intensity of each track in the software's graphic-editing window. Name each track before you record. The soundbites recorded to a track called "voc" should then be labeled automatically in chronological order (for example, "voc_01," "voc_02," "voc_03"). Keep the window that displays these individual takes in view. As you use different takes from different tracks in your final edit, it will be easy to see which soundbites you're using and where they're located.

After you've recorded all of the vocal takes and confirmed that you have at least one good version of each section, create a new vocal track named, for example, "LV Comp" (for "Lead Vocal Comp"). Assign it to the same output with the same effects as the others. Listen to all of the takes of the first section (Verse 1, for example) and choose the best performance. Include the breaths in front of the soundbite so the resulting edit will sound natural. Highlight this soundbite on the original track and copy it. Now paste it to the same location on your comp track but don't remove it from the original. (You may want to refer to the original material later.) Move on to the next section of the tune and repeat this process. If you don't have a good take of a complete section, you'll have to copy smaller soundbites from different takes.

Sometimes you might have to paste individual words or even syllables from different tracks into a comp track, and when this occurs, there are a few tricks you can use to make the edits seamless. If the level is slightly different from one word to the next, use a plug-in or automation to change the gain of the weaker soundbite.

If the timing is inconsistent between takes, isolate the soundbite that is out of time and nudge it earlier or later. If a word or part of a word is slightly out of tune, don't tune the whole take. Make a copy of the offending word, correct it with a pitch-shifting plug-in, and paste the result into your comp track.

Once you have the best takes pasted together, listen to the entire comp in solo and eliminate any stray noises and bad edit points. Examine the entire track and create very small crossfades between the adjoining regions to eliminate digital pops. If you are quick and careful, the singer may not even notice your work, and that means you've done a great job.

Make Mine Hot
Getting Your Best Level
By David Darlington

Many of us who grew up recording to analog tape learned that you must get a good volume level to tape in order to minimize hiss. Analog recording offered a certain warmth and an appealing compression if the level was a little too hot; even distortion was a desirable side effect in some instances. But now that many of us are recording on digital media, we must revisit the level issue. How hot is *too* hot? Is it still important to get a hot level even though there is no tape hiss to worry about?

The answer is a resounding "Yes!" It is extremely important to get maximum levels when recording to a digital medium. The hotter the recorded signal, the larger the digital "words" used to sample the sound. A larger word length (*bit depth*) translates to better sound reproduction. You can experiment yourself when recording something like a guitar or vocal. First, record a track with a very safe level, and then record another take at a level close to the peak. On playback, match the output levels of the two recordings and compare the quality. You'll hear a stunning difference between the two. It's hard to describe, but hotter tracks sound more immediate and "in your face," whereas lower-level tracks sound a bit distant and less distinct. I believe so strongly in hot signals that I am willing to record a track so close to peak that I occasionally go over. I would rather ask an artist to re-sing a phrase or two that went over peak than have a wimpy-sounding vocal for the entire record.

So what does going over the red line sound like? Well, in the days of analog recording, an engineer could get away with quite a bit of peak indication. As long as the tape didn't distort, the change in the recorded sound was minimal. Yet, since most analog meters measure *average* volume, the peaks of *transients* (or attacks) were often undetected by the meter. So, as an analog engineer, one learned to recognize sounds containing a lot of transients—such as hi-hats and crash cymbals—and record them at lower levels so they wouldn't distort on tape.

Today, the digital meters in our workstations react much more quickly and often show transient peaks. This is very helpful, and you should never let these peaks go over 0 VU. There is really no such thing as recording "over" digital 0 VU, since a computer has no way to represent over 0 as a binary number. Instead, it simply reads digital overs as zeroes, shaving off all of the samples that are louder than zero going in. This process is known as *clipping*, and it results in flat spots on the wave at peak points. The sound of a flat peak in playback is very grainy, unpleasant, and distorted—it should be avoided at all costs.

Notice that any audio that peaked during recording won't show as peak on playback because a digital audio workstation cannot record anything above zero. Don't let your

DAT machine fool you—if you saw a peak while recording, the clip is there, but it won't show up when you play it back. Even though you can't see it, the sound quality is compromised.

One other note about peak meters in digital workstations: They are calibrated with the musician/engineer in mind. That is to say, they often show peak or 0 VU slightly before the digital limit is exceeded. Manufacturers purposely build in these pre-peak indicators to save us from ourselves. I've noticed that my ProTools software indicates a peak before my Apogee AD-8000 shows any samples over. (The Apogee can be set to indicate the number of samples clipped by the 0 VU limit, and it's extremely accurate.)

So the challenge is to record maximum signal without clipping in order to get the best possible recorded sound. Now that I think about it, this has always been one of the biggest issues facing engineers, and the really good ones figure it out. Things haven't changed that much after all.

Mind over Meters
A Guide to Setting Levels—Part 1
By Pat Kirtley

Setting audio levels for recording has a lot in common with driving a car. Both activities require accurate judgment and careful awareness. While driving, there is one dashboard gauge we consult often—the speedometer. Speedometers are necessary because the correct driving speed keeps changing, and it's almost impossible to tell how fast you are going just by looking out the window. You would think that after having experienced moving vehicles since childhood, we would develop a natural sense for judging speeds, but except in a very general way, we don't. Reading the speedometer becomes essential, and if we are to abide by the speed limits and negotiate changing conditions, its readings must be accurate.

In the audio world, setting levels properly is equivalent to driving a car at the right speed. Instead of contending with varying road conditions and speed limits, here we encounter constantly changing signal sources. Similar to our inability to judge speed by eye is the hopelessness of trying to determine critical audio levels by ear. For that we need meters—accurate ones—and we must learn how to interpret what they tell us. To make things more interesting, in multitrack recording we must monitor the levels of several audio sources at once.

While critical level setting has always been important, the demands of digital audio have significantly reduced the allowable error margin. The old advice to "just keep those needles out of the red" that served novices for so many years won't cut it anymore. In pure analog recording, it didn't usually matter if the meter needles went into the red zone now and then—you would probably still get a usable recording. With digital we must be more cautious about over-levels. Distortion caused by over-recorded levels is one of the things that cannot be corrected after the fact.

When you consider the complexity of the mixing process, it becomes clear that an incorrect level-setting strategy will be compounded when many individual recordings (tracks) come together for the final mix. In digital recording, cumulative errors become a serious problem, threatening to degrade the integrity of any recording. To form a strategy for level setting, we must become educated in several areas of audio technology. And it's worth mentioning here that all of the considerations about proper recording levels go ditto for the process of sampling. Though the recording times are measured in milliseconds instead of minutes, correct level setting is just as crucial in the sampling world.

Squeezing the Real World into a Box

When we record sounds from the real, physical world into any electronic form, we are trying to squeeze them into an imperfect form that has "less of everything" than the world from which they came. The better the recording channel, the bigger the "box" we have to work with, but all recording channels have limits. Two demons we constantly face in recording are *noise* and *distortion*; noise is the result of levels set too low and distortion is the result of levels set too high. Good recordings (level-wise, at least) are ones that fit the audio program into the middle of this space without rubbing shoulders with the demons. Accurate management of recording levels is the method by which we achieve that goal.

Good Tools

We need good tools to help us for several reasons. First of all, our ears are almost useless in making fine adjustments of audio levels for recording. "Turn it up" or "turn it down" is not good enough. We need to use accurate meters and learn how to interpret what they tell us. Second, our real-world audio sources are rarely constant—they vary wildly in intensity, and we must develop strategies to tame and capture them in usable form. To begin learning the tools of the trade, we must know how to measure audio levels, both electronically and acoustically.

We must also learn how to use our ears as tools. With conscientious practice, the recordist can learn to hear things that others don't. Human ears can never be perfect meters, but they can become exquisitely sensitive in terms of comparing the level of one channel with another, and hearing the grating fringe of distortion when it begins to occur.

Characteristics of Sound Sources and Recording Channels

Four important criteria describe the qualities relating to level. They are *dynamic range*, *headroom*, *peak-to-average ratio*, and *loudness*.

Dynamic range is the ratio of loudest sound peaks to softest audible sounds in a recording or live performance. Some real-life sound sources have greater dynamic range than what can be recorded on a given recording channel. In recording channels, dynamic range is potentially limited by the *noise floor* on the soft end, and by maximum recordable level on the loud end. Instruments such as flute, sax, voices, and bass have a relatively small dynamic range, and those such as piano, percussion kits, and acoustic guitar can have a much greater one. Musical ensembles present a more complex dynamic range picture. In general, the larger the ensemble, in terms of number of sound sources, the greater the dynamic range it presents. A symphony orchestra can pose the greatest challenge for recordists in terms of dynamic range—the full orchestra might be playing one minute, and then just one solo instrument the next.

Headroom is the amount of signal an electronic channel can handle beyond the highest average level without producing distortion. This term is more often used to describe amplification channels than recording channels. A simple way to define headroom is to say that it is the amount that a signal can exceed zero on the meters without distorting. In digital recording channels the concept of headroom has little meaning, since digital meters normally do not register above zero and exceeding that level results in a completely distorted recording. But in working with consoles and mixers, headroom is a critical factor.

Peak-to-average ratio is the ratio of the average program level (sometimes called the *RMS level*) and the tip-top of the loudest peaks. The peak-to-average characteristic is the way we define how much "weight" a signal carries. Here is a way to visualize the concept. The *relative loudness* of a signal—the way your ear makes a judgment of loudness—is based on the average power of the signal. But the peaks of the signal, which may stand up much higher than the average level, are what determine how hard the signal can be pushed through the recording channel. Ultimately, a signal with a low peak-to-average ratio can sound louder because we can record it at a higher level without distortion problems. The strategies of limiting and compression have grown up from the desire to raise the average level of a signal while reducing the height of the peaks.

Recordists need to learn which sound sources have high peak-to-average ratios, because these are the most challenging ones to record. Live sound sources inevitably have higher ratios than prerecorded ones, because there is a good chance that whoever recorded a sound the first time already did something in the way of level management or compression to tame the high-ratio sources. I mention this because there are lots of second-generation sources to be found, ranging from prerecorded tracks from another studio, to instrument samples played back from a keyboard. First-generation sources that can be problematic are piano, acoustic guitar (and most other plucked acoustic stringed instruments), drum kit, percussion kit, and many sound effects.

Do not confuse peak-to-average ratio with *dynamic range*. The peak-to-average ratio exists even for one note produced by a source, while dynamic range considers the range or intensity over time, comparing how loud a source plays at its loudest and softest times. For a given source, the peak-to-average ratio is relatively constant.

Loudness is the only aspect of recorded sound that is better judged by the ear than by meters and computer displays. Loudness is the subjective intensity of a sound source. We almost always consider loudness in a relative way. Our ears' judgment of absolute sound intensity is terrible, but our sense of comparing the loudness of one sound with that of another is amazingly sensitive. The most experienced recording engineers record by using accurate metering, but they mix by ear! In fact, meters are lousy indicators of perceived loudness, and of all the meter designs there have been, modern digital peak meters are the most useless in this respect.

The human ear completely disregards short-term peaks when judging loudness. Maddeningly, they are the same short transients that cause the meters on your DAT machine to flash "OVER" if your levels are set a little too high. So it's a great paradox that something we can hardly detect by ear causes us the most problems in level setting.

Also, the human ear is very sensitive to relative tonal balance. We are more responsive to the loudness of mid- and high-frequency sounds, and much less responsive to low bass. It's not a deficiency—it's just that eons ago, Mother Nature designed the ear to emphasize speaking voices and danger signals. Music came a lot later in the game. In many contemporary music styles, we like to hear bass frequencies—this range is where we sense the "power" of the music—so we tend to jack up the bass in our recordings. But level meters (and recording machines) are designed to respond equally at all frequencies. They just don't care about this human hearing curve. The result is that as we increase the proportion of low end using EQ settings, we create program signals that creep higher on the level meter readings, even though we didn't touch the faders. Adding EQ is just like turning up the volume on a particular range of frequencies. Any frequency range that we emphasize, if it contains significant audio energy, will cause an overall level increase.

Metering

Since our ears are fairly inaccurate when it comes to quantifying sound levels, the only realistic way to measure and monitor audio levels is with visual indicators—using our eyes instead of our ears. Meters come in many shapes and sizes and, like everything else, with varying degrees of quality and accuracy.

In the early days of audio, standards were developed for metering. For many years the standard meter was called a *VU meter*, and the audio industry maintained exacting specifications for its construction and performance. VU stands for *volume units*, and recording professionals became very familiar with the characteristics of these meters. Since the meter apparatus itself was mechanical, there was a significant delay in its response to quick transient sounds and peaks, so that a short burst of sound would register far below its true level. Instead of being a fault, this sluggishness factor was eventually standardized and allowed the meters to respond to real-life audio programs in a way that matched, to a high degree, the way human hearing perceives loudness. The response of the meter made intuitive sense to the user. For many years, the familiar standard meter face with its needle swinging across markings—from a lower limit of –20VU to an in-the-red +3VU—was a clear roadmap that guided engineers' level-setting decisions.

As electronics became more sophisticated in the 1970s, a new idea was added alongside the VU meter: the *peak indicator light*. This light, which readily utilized the newly developed LED (light-emitting diode), could respond to signal peaks hundreds of times faster than a meter mechanism could. The combination of an "average-reading" VU meter and peak LED (which could be calibrated not just to show the occurrence of peak overloads, but also to measure their intensity) was an excellent approach. Many engineers would never wish for anything more.

LEDs in Digitalville

Digital audio changed everything. Not only was the noise level in recording systems reduced so that musically significant sounds occurring below –20VU required attention, but the territory above zero became a forbidden land. This required a new approach to metering. The standard VU meter, after a long and dependable career in thousands of studios, began to be abandoned because its range wasn't wide enough and its scale of –20 to +3 seemed irrelevant to digital demands. The first digital meters tried to mimic the activity of VU meters. They were simply multi-segmented clusters of peak-reading LEDs set to fire off at different levels. These meters are still with us, and have varying degrees of accuracy, precision, and range. A typical meter of this type has maybe seven segments, which illuminate at –40, –20, –10, –5, –3, –1, and 0.

There are problems with multi-segment peak indicators. While they can be accurate in their calibration, unless they are driven by fairly sophisticated circuitry, the movement of their light patterns doesn't relate well to what we hear, which was the most admirable characteristic of the old VU meter. Also, the meters often don't have enough segments to give the illusion of smooth movement. Manufacturers tend to shortchange the user here because more segments equals greater cost, and in low-dollar equipment there have been some nasty compromises. Sometimes your only metering reference is a set of hard-to-read markings on a tiny, slow-responding, multipurpose liquid crystal display. It is a paradox: Detailed accurate meters are crucial to good recording, but in the most sophisticated home-recording environment the world has ever known, a good meter is hard to find.

So how do you get a good meter? One way is to purchase a dedicated metering unit. There are wonderful external meters produced by companies such as Dorrough, Mytek, and Logitek that are electronic versions of the most effective analog and digital metering styles ever designed. Instead of five or seven segments, they have dozens to hundreds, and incorporate peak-hold readings with an average responding display—a visual combination that makes intuitive sense to the user.

Dedicated meters are fairly expensive, but they are a good long-term investment if you plan to get serious about your recording work. Much less expensive, and still highly accurate, are the virtual meters built into quality computer audio software. With these, the software designer can create metering systems entirely from programming code, and is limited only by his or her skills and imagination to create useful meter displays. Many of the top-quality desktop audio software systems have useful and highly versatile metering options.

Mind over Meters
A Guide to Setting Levels—Part 2
By Pat Kirtley

Part 1 examined some of the basics of setting levels. Further information will be provided here, as well as some hands-on exercises you can use to probe the limits of recording-channel capabilities for yourself, and some real-world strategies you can use to approach every level-setting situation like a pro.

Over and Out

Setting levels on digital recording equipment and computer-based workstations has introduced a new factor with which the recordist must contend: the *digital over* or *clipping* indicator. Many pieces of audio equipment use clip indicators to let the user know when internal levels have exceeded the circuit's capacity, or when an amplifier has reached the limits of its clean output. The message they transmit is simple and clear: "Back off!" And we do, and everything is okay again.

But the over indicator on a digital recorder has a somewhat different meaning. When it flashes (or trips, requiring a reset action), it means that for some fraction of time exceeding a couple of samples, all of the available bits have been used up. Beyond that point, no information is recorded, so the resulting waveform has its top chopped off very cleanly. The resulting sharp edges can sound very nasty on playback.

To make matters more confusing, when you play back the tape, the meters give no indication that an over occurred. Why? Digital recording meters stop at "0" and have no markings above that point. When you clip the signal, no recording takes place higher than the "0" level. So you see what appears to be a good, healthy recording that kicks the meters pretty hard and has no apparent problems. This is why you must respect what the over indicator tells you *during* recording. When it trips, you really don't know how high above zero the signal was trying to go. If it was a significant peak, you will hear it later, and it *can't* be fixed in the mix.

How audible are digital overs? Do they always destroy an otherwise good take? The answer is that they are sometimes just barely detectable by ear, and no, they don't necessarily ruin the recording. If just a few cycles of a signal peak are involved, the clipping may not be audible at all, but large hunks of sound that push past the top limit may sound horrendous upon playback. Always use your ears, and don't take "maybe" for an answer. My acid test is that if I can hear a peak distortion problem upon playback in a digital recording channel, then I need to re-record the track at a lower level.

Adjusting Gain Stages in the Mixer

Mixer design is based on *gain stages*. As the signal makes its way through the mixer, correct levels must be established at specific points to minimize distortion and noise. The places where the signal can be controlled are: the *input stage* (also known as the mic preamp), the *mix stage*, and the *output stage*. The controls at these points are, respectively, the trim control, the channel fader, and the master fader. Some mixers and consoles have more gain stages than these three, but these three points, at least, are present on nearly every mixer.

The procedure for setting up the gain stages is straightforward and should be followed unless you are working with an abnormal signal source. First, set the trim control to its lowest setting. Next, set the output level and channel fader controls to the nominal setting point established by the mixer manufacturer. In most cases, this will be the "0 dB" point and is about three-quarters of the way toward the maximum setting of the control. Many designers put a *detent*—a stopping point that you can feel—at the spot. Some manufacturers use the midpoint of the control as the "0" setting.

Next, with the signal you are going to record connected to the mixer's input, increase the trim control until the mixer's output stage meters peak around 0 dB. If you have multiple sound sources, repeat this setting process with each channel independently. If you have only one set of meters, as is the case with many small mixers, mute all of the other channels except the one you are working on. On a larger console with a meter for each fader channel, you may set the working level using the channel meters.

When all of the sources are combined, the level at the output stage may be considerably higher, and can be controlled by reducing the master fader setting. The above procedure is one that will give good results in general, but if the manufacturer of your mixer recommends something different, it's best to follow their instructions.

Digital Resolution

Earlier we said that recording is like stuffing things from the real world into a smaller space. That's a good way to think of digital recording channels—as virtual storage space. This real estate is divided into elementary chunks called *bit levels*. The more bit levels we have, the higher the digital resolution. The idea of resolution can be easily understood by anyone who has seen a computer picture magnified. Computer pictures are made up of blocks called pixels. The bit-level steps in digital audio are equivalent to visual pixels. If the pixels are too big, or if we don't have enough of them, or if we blow up the picture so that the pixels are magnified, it looks increasingly blocky and "unreal." If the blocks are sufficiently small, they become invisible, and we see only the information from the picture itself.

In 16-bit digital recording, we have approximately 65,000 bit levels to work with. It seems like plenty of blocks, and you might think we wouldn't have to worry about a resolution problem. The trouble begins if we set the overall record level too low. A lower recording level means fewer bit levels are used, and if the resulting recording is later raised up to normal levels, it's the sonic equivalent of magnifying a digital image. The blocks begin to show—or in this case, be heard. The current movement toward 20-bit digital (more than one million bit levels instead of 65,000) and even 24-bit (16 million levels!) is driven by the desire to be free of resolution limitations.

A rule of thumb is to set the recording level of digital channels as high as possible without running into digital overs or clipping. One way to achieve this is to use −12 dB rather than 0 dB as your target level, thereby leaving a margin of 12 dB for signal peaks while still maintaining a healthy amount of average signal. Many recording pros use this method and get consistently good results.

Going over Big

Train your ear to hear distortion and noise. I can't think of a better way to do this than to create your own experimental havoc by running various levels too high (or low) on purpose and listening to the result. You won't do any permanent damage, and you will develop a familiarity with various aberrations, which can help you to avoid them in real-life recording situations. For input sources in these experiments, you can use prerecorded tracks. If you have a willing live-source performer, that's even better.

First, try some mixer distortion. With the channel gain and main output set lower than normal, raise the input trim control up until you hear the sound getting a rough edge, and then bring it up even further until you hear that really hell-raising grind. Not pretty, is it? You can get a healthy dose of crud going even though the master output levels are in the "normal" range.

It will help even more if you run the levels on your monitor system lower than normal when you do this listening test. Why? Because at loud levels, your hearing subconsciously expects something to distort and prepares for this. Distortion is less surprising at loud listening levels, but hearing distortion at very low monitoring levels makes it obvious that the problem is coming from somewhere other than the monitoring system.

Next, after resetting your mixer so that the output is crystal clear, make an intentionally over-level recording on a digital recording device—a DAT, minidisc, or computer workstation—by raising its input levels. You will notice that where you had to push the mixer electronics fairly hard to get the sound to go ragged, the digital recorder went into rancid territory rather easily. Bring up the level to where it trips the over indicator, and then go a little farther. Next, record another section with the input set even higher. You may not hear any distress while you are making the recording—many digital recording channels use purely analog monitoring means—but when you play it back, you get to hear firsthand what hard digital clipping sounds like. It is an interesting exercise, and in doing it you will gain a better appreciation for that "over" light.

Lastly, make an intentionally under-level recording. This is so that you can find out what's going on at the low-level end of the process, where hiss and lack of bit resolution become apparent. Record a passage with the meters showing no higher than about −30 dB. This is a very low level, and on some machines the input meters will barely register it. When you play it back, you will need to bring your monitor levels up higher to hear things normally, and that's when you get to hear all of the bottom-feeding artifacts that are always present but are usually masked by louder information. Besides educating your ear to the qualities of noise and insufficient bit levels, this test magnifies the differences in quality between various machines and digital encoders/decoders. Some machines do much better than others in this test, and if yours still sounds pretty good with peaks at −30, it is a better-than-average recording channel.

Back in the Real World

To become a better recordist in terms of managing levels, start using good tools—accurate, calibrated meters—and learn how to understand them so that they become trusted friends. Your other reliable resource is critical listening. Develop a discriminating ear—one that is always alert for sounds that aren't quite right. At regular intervals, a good recordist turns attention away from the enjoyable musical qualities of a recording and consciously listens for the bad stuff. By listening for undesirable artifacts, you can learn how to avoid creating them.

Always remember the "three bears" approach to setting levels: There will always be a correct setting for any program source and for any particular recording device that is not too hot and not too cold, but *just right*. A good recordist is one who knows how to find exactly that spot.

Tips for Successful Level Setting

Prerecorded Material, Two-Track Transfers

- Digital to Digital: No level setting required. Digital to digital transfers are merely copying bits, just like a computer copies files from disk to disk. This only applies in cases where there is a digital-only connection between devices (e.g., AES-EBU, S/PDIF, optical fiber).

- Analog to Digital: Do a run-through and observe the meters. Set the highest peak just below 0 dB.

- Digital to Analog: On most digital systems, it is possible to do a run-through and let the system find the highest peak point in the source material. Next, play that passage into the analog recorder for level setting at near 0 dB (or, depending on machine and tape type, at +2 to +4). Then, rewind everything and make the transfer.

Recording New Material—Studio/Digital Record Channels

Make sure the mic preamp levels are set properly; this is the console stage where distortion is most likely to occur. Next, set recording input levels. Hopefully, you can run through the performance at least once without recording. Pay close attention to peak-producing areas. Use the best meters you can get your hands on, and make sure that they are accurately calibrated before the session. It is a challenge to monitor the record levels on many channels at once. In a multitrack tracking session, you can avoid being overwhelmed if you set sources a little lower in general to avoid maxing them out, and turn your attention to critical, dynamic sources during the session—particularly drums, percussive sources, and vocals. Try to get recorded peaks at about –1 on recorder input meters. If overs occur, immediately play back that section to make sure you can live with the result.

Recording New Material—Field Recordings

Without a chance to "run through" a performance in advance, a more conservative approach is called for. Set mic preamps at moderate levels. Set maximum recording levels at –3 or less on the meters. Resist the urge to "ride levels," and don't worry about the occasional over-peak that will inevitably occur. If you are recording an extremely high-level program source (rock band, etc.), consider using a –10 dB pad at the microphone to stop excessive levels before they get to the preamp stage. Digital overs do not necessarily condemn the quality of the recording. Depending on the nature of the program source and the length of the actual overload, the result may be tolerable, or even inaudible. Don't assume a couple of over-peaks have ruined your recording.

Effects

Coping with Compressors
Demystifying Those Dynamic Controllers
By David Darlington

Compression is one of the more frequently misunderstood aspects of engineering, particularly for those just starting out. Everyone has heard that compressors are necessary and useful, but novice mixers seldom have a clear picture of what these devices do electronically, and the sonic effects of compressors are often misunderstood. They're called compressors because they compress the *dynamic range* (i.e., the softest to the loudest parts) of the audio signal. This can have an important effect on not just the full mix, but on the loudest and softest parts of a single sound, such as a snare drum. Let's look at the basic functions of a simple compressor.

A compressor is basically an amplifier that passes an audio signal through untouched until it reaches a certain level. This level is called the *threshold*, and it is one of the most important parameters to adjust when compressing. It determines at what point the compressor kicks in and starts doing its job. The amplifier then restricts volume above the threshold by a certain ratio—another important parameter to consider.

For example, if the ratio is 2:1, then for every two decibels of increase in the input signal, the output signal will increase by only one. Similarly, with a 4:1 ratio, an increase of four at input will result in an increase of only one at output, and so on. You can compress all the way up to infinity (∞), which means that no amount of increase in the sound will raise the level of the output. This is sometimes referred to as *brick wall limiting,* because the signal level hits a wall (i.e., threshold) that it cannot cross. In fact, the term *limiting* means this type of compression—i.e., the level is restricted to this threshold level and cannot go higher.

On more advanced compressors, there are additional controls to refine the action of the amplifier even further. The most common of these are the attack and release controls, which function much the same way as the ADSR controls on your favorite analog synth.

The *attack* parameter determines how long the compressor waits to react once it senses the threshold has been crossed. A fast attack setting will react quickly, keeping the peak level from coming through. A slower attack will allow transient peaks to come through the circuit and then lower the volume of the later signal. Likewise, a quick release will let go of the volume once it returns below the threshold, while a slow release will continue to reduce the level even though the input is no longer above the threshold. You can use these tools to your advantage to sculpt sounds by making the compressor react in different ways to sharp attack transients and long, sustained tones.

Another parameter you may see on your compressor's faceplate is a *knee switch*, which toggles between *hard* and *soft* knee. If you look at a graph of a sound's input versus its output, it smoothly increases at a 1:1 ratio until it passes the threshold point. Here it bends to follow the ratio of compression; this bend is called the knee because it looks just like a bent knee. A hard knee changes immediately from a 1:1 ratio to your compression ratio, while a soft knee makes the transition more gradually.

Finally, a very helpful control on many compressors is the *make-up control*. If you've already set up a mix or gotten an optimum recording level, and then decided to add compression—which in most cases will reduce the overall volume of the signal—the make-up control will allow you to bring it back to its unprocessed level.

Most listeners can sense an increase in punchiness when a sound is compressed—which can be great for your mix, but be careful! Overcompression can suck the life out of any sound (or mix) and make it small and thin. I always keep an eye on my compressors to make sure that they are not working too hard. The needles or LEDs should show some movement but not massive amounts, unless that's what you're going for. Use your ears, and keep notes about your discoveries. You'll soon be the master of your compressors.

Compression
By Julian McBrowne

Next to a reverb unit, the most important outboard effect in a home studio is the compressor. The compressor evens out levels, gives mixes a punchy sound, and can prevent loud signals from distorting and soft ones from picking up inherent noise. Like good film directing, good compression is transparent. Because of this, compression techniques can be difficult to master. You may not be aware of good compression, but you can always tell when bad compression occurs.

Even if you don't own a compressor, you've probably done some compression on your own just setting levels. You're recording a vocal, and you ask the singer to sing a bit so you can get levels. You bring up your input fader until you start to see something on the meter, and you keep going up until the signal gets too hot—then you bring it down, searching for that elusive point where the loud stuff doesn't go onto the red, and the soft stuff doesn't just disappear.

In fact, you'll never get the perfect level with a stationary input fader. You have to move it up to catch the soft stuff, and back it down to keep the loudest stuff from overloading. Congratulations, you're *riding gain*, an exercise that requires anticipation, quick reflexes, and ESP. It can work for a vocal recording, but what about all of those other instruments with changing levels? Guitar, bass, drum, and keyboard sounds all move faster than you could ever respond to them. Enter the compressor.

Simply put, what a compressor does is turn down the loudest parts of a given signal, thus reducing its dynamic range. Once you've squashed the loud peaks, you're then able to increase the volume of the entire signal. As a result, not only are the loud parts softer, but the soft parts are now louder. However, you must be careful not to overcompress, or you could reduce your track to a thin imitation of its former self. It all depends on how you set the controls.

Most full-featured compressors have the following five controls.

Threshold

This sets the level where gain reduction starts to happen. The lower the threshold, the more the signal will be subject to compression.

Ratio

This tells the compressor how to scale down the signals that exceed the threshold. Compression ratios are expressed with two numbers. The first refers to the input and the second to the output. A 1:1 ratio causes no compression at all. At 2:1, signals that are input into the compressor above the threshold are subject to a 50 percent gain reduction. For example, a snare drum hit that is 4 dB above the threshold would be only 2 dB over when it came out of the compressor. The higher the ratio, the more drastic the gain reduction. Set at its highest ratio, a compressor will function as a limiter and not allow any signal to pass that's louder than the threshold. Generally speaking, high ratio and low threshold settings give the most obvious kinds of compression. Low ratios and high thresholds are usually smoother.

Attack

This determines how soon gain reduction will start after the signal crosses the threshold. Short attack times cause every peak to trigger gain reduction. Setting this for 25 to 50 ms will allow you to compress drum and bass sounds without killing their punch.

Release

This setting determines how long the gain reduction will last. Fast release times restore the level quickly, longer times can make some sounds seem to last longer.

Output

This controls the overall output of the unit. Use it to turn up your newly compressed signal.

Some units have a much more limited set of controls. If you have an input control instead of a threshold knob, your compressor probably has a fixed threshold and a variable input. Other units feature automatic attack and release controls and don't allow the user to set these parameters. Most units have some kind of input/output metering, but the most useful meter on any compressor is the one that shows gain reduction, since it shows what's really happening to the signal.

To illustrate how a compressor works, let's use as an example a rhythm guitar part with a wide dynamic range. Let's say it includes some picking (on the soft side), some stroked chords (average volume), and some funky chord chops (on the loud side). We'll begin with the threshold control set as high as possible, and the ratio set to 3:1. With an eye on the gain reduction meter and an ear to the monitors, we'll lower the threshold until the funky guitar chops cause about 3 dB of gain reduction. The softer picking and chording shouldn't cause any gain reduction since they fall below the threshold. Our final move will be to raise the output control by 3 dB. The end result should be a track where everything sounds louder and smoother.

Tube-style compression and softknee threshold features, which you'll find on some units, can help you achieve smooth and undetectable gain reduction. If you really want to squeeze the signal for an effect, try setting the threshold very low and then experiment with different ratios. For an example of some serious vocal compression, check out Alanis Morrisette's "Hand in My Pocket." Notice that the breaths between the lines are almost as loud as the lyrics. Obvious compression, in this instance, makes the vocal very intense, very loud, and very effective.

(Sonic) Barbarians at the Gate
"Quiet Down Out There!"
By David Darlington

The noise gate is one of the most helpful components of your outboard processing gear or the dynamics section on your digital mixer. It's also one of the simplest to use. Noise gates do what any gate is expected to do: open to let something through and then shut when it has passed. In the case of your system, the sound of the instrument or voice is let through while rumble, hiss, or other objectionable noise is barred from your mix (this assumes, of course, that the sound of the instrument is louder than the noise you're trying to control). Gates are especially helpful in controlling analog tape hiss, and they can also be used in a number of creative ways to alter sounds.

There are usually five controls on a gate: *threshold, attack, hold, release,* and *range.*

Threshold refers to the level that must be present before the gate is opened. If the level is too low—thus allowing quieter sounds to pass through—then the gate may not really be helping you filter unwanted noise. On the other hand, if it is set too high, then parts of the sound that you want to hear may be removed. Listen to the track in solo and adjust the threshold level until the gate opens easily whenever the sound is present. Be especially careful on sounds with lots of transient impact like drums, percussion, and pianos. Improper threshold levels can rob these sounds of the attacks that help our ears identify them, resulting in a mix that lacks punch and sparkle.

The attack, hold, and release settings operate much like the envelope on a synthesizer. Attack is the length of time it takes for the gate to spring open. Usually a short time is desirable to make sure that the gate allows the full sound to pass through, but a slow attack can sometimes be helpful. For example, you may want to take the snap off the front of a sampled kick drum to make it sound warmer. But be careful not to make the attack too short, or a popping sound could result each time the gate opens.

Hold is a duration setting, usually expressed in milliseconds, that determines how long the gate will stay open. You'll want shorter values for things like snare and kick drums and longer values for cymbals and pianos. This control can be used creatively to make a long snare drum sound much shorter (the famous *gated snare*) or to make a reverb tail stop abruptly for an unusual effect (the equally famous *gated reverb*). Set this value for a duration that's a bit longer for sounds that have a lot of dynamic range, such as piano or vocals. If the gate does not stay open long enough, the ends of phrases can be clipped and natural noises like breath can be lost. Sometimes this is desirable—for example, in a loud rock vocal where there is a lot of leakage from drums and guitar amps. But in a soft ballad, you really don't want to hear the gate.

The release control also represents a time value, referring to the amount of time that the gate will take to close after the hold time has elapsed. The hold and release times work in conjunction to sculpt the end of the sound that's being gated. If you are removing noise from a reverb return, you will want a long release to allow the natural tail of the reverb to pass through. If you are truncating a snare sound to make it very short, then a small release time is appropriate. Again, listen to the sound in solo and shape it with a combination of hold and release times until it sounds natural and the unwanted noise is removed.

The range control sets the strength or dynamic range of the gate. Lower settings mean that the gate is not closing all of the way down, allowing some sound to pass through even below the threshold. As the range is increased, the gate closes further until, at maximum range, it is fully closed.

Some gates have an external or *sidechain* input, allowing the sound to be shaped by another source. For example, the kick drum could control the bass guitar so that each time the kick strikes, the gate on the bass opens up. This would effectively make them seem "tighter" in their performance. You can send a low oscillator (like 50 Hz) through a gate and then control it with the kick drum sound, thereby adding what's called an *808* to the existing kick. Another useful application of a noise gate is to decrease the "roominess" on things like toms and cymbals. By lightly gating these sounds with a medium release, you can take out some of the background ambience while still maintaining the original sound.

Noise gates are your allies in controlling unwanted noise in your mix and, like all friends, they should not be mistreated. Don't gate everything and don't gate too strongly or you will suck the life out of your mix. Just use gates to help tame that unruly crowd.

Stir of Echoes
Reverb Revealed
By David Darlington

Electronic reverb is the result of many overlapping delays designed to simulate the reflections in a specific acoustic space. The larger the space, the longer the delays take to return and thus the longer the reverberation. Digital reverb designers separate the types of spaces they emulate into four major categories. *Halls* are the largest-sized spaces, while *rooms*, or *chambers*, are smaller spaces. *Plate* reverb emulates the sound of a metallic plate resonating to an input signal, while *non-linear* or *gated* reverb is not a space at all but a man-made sound. These various reverb categories are programmed using complex algorithms to send the many delays crashing into each other and repeating randomly so as to fool the ear into believing the sound exists in a certain space.

So, the first question to ask when applying reverb to a sound is "Where should this sound exist?" In the early days of close-mic recording, music was actually sent to a chamber (like a stairwell or basement) in which another mic was placed, creating an "echo chamber." Later, someone figured out that you could get a similar effect by rattling a metal plate with your music and then miking the sound of the rattling plate. This "plate" reverb is still in use today and many engineers prefer this sound on drums, brass, and especially vocals. Of course, strings and orchestral instruments are usually heard in halls, whereas percussion instruments sound good in smaller rooms.

The main parameter that controls the overall sound of the reverb is called *decay*. Decay, or *reverb time*, refers to the length of the reverb tail and is usually expressed in seconds or milliseconds. Rooms are short, ranging from .04 to two seconds, while halls are longer at anywhere from one to five seconds or more. Plates fall somewhere in between. Apply the reverb to your sound and try playing with the decay parameter. You'll find that by shortening the tail, you can add more reverb to the sound without sloshing up your mix. Conversely, you can add long reverb very lightly to give the mix a subtle ambience. Some more expensive reverb units divide the tail into three frequency bands, which gives the engineer more control over the color of the tail. If the high frequencies die out earlier than the mids or lows, the reverb will sound warm and fat. If the lows die out before the highs, the effect will be bright and splashy. Once you've settled on a basic length, leave the midrange decay at this duration and experiment with changing the decay of the high and low frequencies. You may have to search for these parameters under different names such as "Bass Multiply" or "Hi Color" depending on the manufacturer, but you're basically altering the decay parameter of specific frequencies.

When you've set the decay and *color* (high and low decay), it's time to examine the *predelay*. Predelay is the length of time it takes for the reverb to start after the initial sound is heard. Many presets come with little or no predelay, but in a musical application this predelay is extremely important. By increasing predelay, you give the sound a separation from the reverb tail that allows it to stay "in your face" and be wet at the same time. Try experimenting with a really large predelay for new and unusual reverb effects. Use a small amount (10 or 20 milliseconds) to separate the music from the reverb. Try a large amount (200 milliseconds) with a small-room reverb to create a spacey ambience. Engineers who use real plate reverb often put a digital delay in line before the plate to create predelay, and the real "old schoolers" use an analog tape slap delay for a super-warm vocal reverb.

Another important component of the reverb sound is called *early reflection*. Early reflections are the first echoes you would hear coming back from the walls in your space. These reflections by themselves do not sound like reverb (they have no "tail" effect) but they do create a sense of space around a sound. Many engineers favor these early reflections over big reverb tails because their mixes can have a lot of early reflections without sounding overly wet. To hear what these reflections do to your sound, turn down the reverb level, increase the number and level of the reflections, and then mix the reverb tail back in sparingly.

Mixers, Mixing, and Mastering

Making Sense of Mixers
Signal Flow Basics
By Jerry Tardif

To the uninitiated, mixers can be quite intimidating. Rows and rows of knobs, buttons, and faders can seem hopelessly complex. However, once you understand the basics of how mixers are configured, you'll discover that they're much simpler than you perhaps first thought. Let's dive right in.

Mixers can usually be divided into two sections: the channel strips and the master section. The number of channel strips generally ranges in groups of four or eight (four, eight, 12, 16, 20, 24, 32, etc.). All channels are usually identical. However, some mixers have two channel types: mono and stereo. This typically occurs on mixers designed for use with stereo sources (keyboards, drum machines, etc.) but, overall, the channels are very similar.

At the top of the strip (or adjacent to it on the back), you'll usually find at least one 1/4" jack for microphones and line inputs. Often there will be a second (XLR) jack, used only for microphones and able to supply phantom power, which many condenser mics need in order to function. Beneath the input jack is the *trim control*, used to adjust the input signal level.

The next set of controls is usually the *auxiliary sends* or the *EQ*. Assuming it's the sends, there may be two, four, or more controls. They allow you to send the channel's signal to effects devices, such as reverb. What's so nice about this arrangement is that it allows every channel needing reverb to access the same processor—you don't need a separate unit for each channel unless you want to use more than one type of reverb. Auxiliary sends can also be used for providing a cue mix to the musicians through their monitors (like at a live gig) or to their headphones. Depending upon how many sends you have, you may be able to provide several different mixes so each musician can hear himself and whatever other instrument he needs most (such as bass and drums).

Often, you'll see a button with one or more send controls that says something like *pre/post* or *PFL/AFL*. This allows the send control to tap its signal before or after the channel fader. Usually, you'll want your effect to follow the fader (post fader) so the ratio of wet to dry signal doesn't change as you adjust the level. Conversely, use the pre setting when sending a cue so a fader adjustment doesn't change the mix sent to the musicians—especially if you're *riding gain* (i.e., adjusting levels during the recording process).

The EQ section is divided into two or more frequency bands. On a basic mixer, the EQ section might consist of only low and high bands, while more expensive boards will also include one or more midrange controls. Generally speaking, the more expensive the mixer, the more EQ options. A higher-priced board might have two midrange bands, each with a selectable center frequency. A more deluxe model might also allow you to control the bandwidth of the boost or cut as well as the center frequency and level, providing true parametric EQ for one or more bands. The best thing is that all of this control is available independently for each channel; this allows you to add more highs to the cymbals here and cut an annoying boomy bass frequency there. You may also find an *EQ bypass* button that allows you to remove the EQ section from the channel with one touch. This is a cool feature because it allows you to compare an equalized signal with a flat one.

The signal then proceeds to the *pan* control, which allows you to determine where it will "sit" in the stereo mix, from full left to full right or anywhere between. Nearby, there will be a *mute* button (which turns the channel off) and a *solo* button (which turns all of the other channels off, leaving just the selected channel on); in this way, you can listen to a single channel to check it for mistakes or to fine-tune the EQ. Usually, you can solo several channels at one time and listen to see what any combination of them will sound like together—all without affecting the mix going to the main channels.

Finally, there's the *fader* or *level* control. Sliding or turning this control allows you to adjust the channel's volume in the overall mix.

Earlier, I avoided mentioning two more jacks that are grouped with the input jacks. An *insert* jack allows you to introduce a *serial effect* (i.e., the entire signal flows through it and is affected). This is different from the auxiliary sends, which are in parallel and allow you to mix some wet signal (for instance, from a reverb or delay unit) with the dry signal. Serial effects are usually compressors, limiters, or gates that operate on the entire signal rather than just a portion of it. *Parallel effects* include not just reverb and delay, but also chorus, flanger, tremolo, and other modulation effects.

The other type of jack you'll find here is the *direct out*, which taps an individual channel's signal after the fader and is independent of the main mix. This often goes to its own track on a multitrack recorder, but it can also be used for another function that requires the processing available in a channel strip, such as preamplification, EQ, or level setting.

Anatomy of a Channel Strip
Out of One, Many
By David Darlington

The first time you see a huge console in a professional recording studio, it can be quite intimidating. What are all of those knobs and switches for anyway? Surprisingly enough, even the biggest behemoth of a console operates much the same as a humble project studio board, or even a DJ mixer for that matter.

Basically the job of a mixer is to collect sounds from various sources, blend them together, and send them back out to various places, either individually or in combinations. The number of sounds that can be included in this blend depends on the number of channels in your mixer. Each channel consists of the same basic building blocks, so even a large console is simply made up of many clones of the same channel strip.

All channels have at their beginning the input, or source connection, and these usually come in two varieties: *mic* and *line*. Mic is obviously for microphones, and line is for almost everything else, including effects processors, tape (or hard-disk) recorders, and other sound sources such as CD players. Some signals such as guitars and basses must be boosted to mic level through a DI (direct injection) box and then connected to the mic input. Most consoles have an *input trim* knob to adjust the level of the input to the proper strength. You want this input level to be as close to 0 VU as possible without overloading the channel.

After the input, the sound is directed to the *fader*, which controls the level of the sound in relation to the other channels of your mix. Usually, the fader is routed to the output of the console where you monitor your mix (via your control room speakers or headphones) and use the faders to balance the various sounds. This routing to the console output is often a switch near the top of the fader marked *L/R* or *mix*. If you disengage this switch, the sound won't go to the main mix. There are other circuits to output the sound to other places (e.g., to a tape recorder); these are called *busses*. Switches to connect the sound to these busses are usually located near the main L/R switch, or way up at the top of the strip. Most project studio boards have four or eight busses, but large consoles have up to 48.

If you have bussed a sound to a tape recorder and removed it from the main mix, you will need a way to hear the sound after it is recorded. This is enabled by the *monitor* knob, or fader, usually right above the large fader. The monitor section corresponds to the channels returning from your tape or hard-disk recorder, so Track 1 would appear on Monitor Fader 1, Track 2 on Monitor Fader 2, etc. If you think about it, you can have twice as many inputs to your mix as you have channels: one sound coming in on the channel input (large fader) and one sound returning from tape on the monitor (small fader).

Above the monitor section is a series of knobs (anywhere from two on a simple mixer to 12 on a complex one) called *auxiliary sends* (or *aux sends*). These sends are called auxiliary, because they are neither the main output (L/R) nor the recording (bus) outputs. They can be used to send the sound to outboard processors, headphones, or anywhere you want a balance different from the one created by the faders. On more expensive consoles, the aux send can be changed from *pre-fader* (before the level of the fader) to *post-fader* (after the level of the fader.) In pre, the amount of aux send will not change if you change the level of the large fader; in post, the level of aux send will change relative to the level of the fader. Often, next to the pre/post switch is a switch marked *mon*. Selecting this switch will send the sound from the monitor fader (instead of the sound from the large fader) to the aux send.

In addition to its routing, the sound can also be processed on most channel strips. The most common processing is *equalization* (or *EQ*), which means changing the frequency characteristics or tone of a sound. Most of us are familiar with treble and bass controls, but many consoles have more sophisticated EQs in each channel, consisting of three or four bands of variable frequency cut and boost. Another available processing function is *dynamic control*, which refers to compression (or expansion) and gating. The dynamics section is typically at the top of the strip, above the equalizer. Some consoles allow you to assign the processors to the channel (large fader) or monitor (small fader).

Don't be afraid of a large, complex mixer. Your console may have another layout, or different switches and routing schemes, but all mixers have this basic format: Sound comes in on input, where it is processed and then routed to the main mix, output busses, or additional auxiliary sends. It is returned from the multitrack device on the monitor inputs. When you understand this, life gets easier, no matter which board you're working on.

Grand Central Station
Your Mixer's Center Section
By David Darlington

It's important to understand the *master output circuit* of your board (commonly called the *center section*, even though it's rarely in the center of semi-pro boards, but rather off to the right) in order to really grasp all of its capabilities and be able to take advantage of them. Take a moment to study the labels of the various controls in your desk's master section, as well as the labels of the inputs and outputs on the rear panel, since features vary widely from manufacturer to manufacturer and model to model. You may have only a few of the features discussed here, or you may have more, but when it's time to upgrade, you'll have a good knowledge of what goodies to look for.

On Center

The most important component of the master section is the *main output*, or *summing bus*, which combines all of the signals going through the faders into one mix and sends this out the main output jacks. This stage of your mix is extremely important because it's the last place to tweak anything before the final version reaches the listener's ears. I generally like to run the master fader wide open and control the overall level with the individual faders. Some engineers push the individual faders up too high, which can result in a mix that's too loud for the tape or CD input. Of course, it's alright to then bring down the overall level with the master fader (that's what it's for, after all), but this is like filling a pumper truck with giant buckets only to pump the water out through a garden hose. It's much more efficient to fill the truck with modest buckets (the individual faders) and pump it out with a full-size hose (a fully open master fader). As your mix progresses, the faders keep getting pushed louder and louder, so try starting at a moderate level—say, –3 VU—on the output when you first push up the music. Now, as you tweak the mix, keep a careful eye on that master output level and work between –3 VU and +2 VU. Believe me, your mix will sound better with the master fader open.

Control Room vs. Fader Level

In addition to the master output fader, your board also has other summing circuits for the auxiliary or effects sends. These knobs may be marked "Aux 1," "Aux 2," or "Effect 1," "Effect 2," etc.—these are overall level controls for the output to the effects. If you have achieved a good blend of the reverbs on various channels but you need to control the total output to the effect unit, this knob will attenuate the total send. The same rules apply as for the master fader. The aux busses sound better when the master aux output is left at zero. Some boards have small EQ circuits so that you can brighten or darken the whole send to the reverb. Try taking out the low end on a master aux send to see if it clears up some muddiness in your sound, or try adding some top to the send to get a bit of sparkle in the mix. EQ on the aux send will result in a different sound than EQ inside the reverb or on the return.

Speaking of returns, how does the reverb get back into the mix? Through those circuits marked *aux returns,* of course. Aux returns used to be a luxury on high-priced boards, but now it's common to have up to four returns on even modest consoles. Patch the output of your effects unit into the return and then control the amount of effect in the mix with this knob. Here, it's okay to turn down the level because this is an input source, not an output. Many boards have mute buttons near the aux returns so that you can mute the reverb to compare your mix with or without reverb. If you're not using the aux return, be sure and keep it muted so that the circuit doesn't add any unnecessary noise to the overall sound.

Your mixing desk may have one more set of returns called *external* or *two-track* that provide returns for your computer, DAT recorder, or CD burner. Some consoles allow these inputs to be integrated into the mix, while some provide them only as an alternate listening input, switching off the main mix when they are selected. Here, you'll have to break out the dreaded owner's manual to see which type you have. The switches near these inputs marked *monitor* select which source is going to your control-room speakers. There should also be a *control room level* knob so that you can control the volume to the speakers without changing the level of the mix. In addition to the control room output, you may also have a *cue* output, which controls levels to the headphone outputs on the back of the console. Finally, on more expensive desks, you may find a *status* section that can change the whole configuration of the board with a single button. *Record* status usually enables channel inputs on the large faders and tape returns on smaller monitor faders, while *mix* means tape returns on the large faders and channel inputs on the small faders. Digital consoles use the status section to choose which page of software is displayed on the faders, like "Level" or "Aux 1 Send" and so on.

Use your center section to optimize the input and output gain structure and you'll hear better results in your mixing. Use the aux sends and returns to route sound around your studio, and remember, always use the right-sized bucket to keep the water flowing.

Mixer Logic—Part 1
Demystifying the Left Side of That Thing with All the Knobs
By Jon Chappell

Mixer Basics

"Look at all of those knobs! How do you understand what they all do?" That's the question most people ask me when they walk into my studio and their eyes fall on the mixer. "I have no idea what they do, but aren't they cool looking?" is my usual response, but it wasn't too long ago when I was asking myself the same question. The mixer is by far the most daunting piece of gear for the new recordist, but it's also the most logical, and one of the most important devices in your studio.

All signals must pass through the mixer, whether you're laying down basic tracks, recording an overdub, flying in effects, or mixing down to stereo. Though its function is simply to route signals and apply EQ and effects, the mixer's power and versatility can be intimidating until you understand it. Then, the mixer becomes your closest hardware friend, and you'll be able to read it like a book.

Conceptually, it's easiest to mentally divide a mixer into two parts. The left side—the big one—houses the channels, and each channel is identical in design to the others. Understand one, and you understand all eight, 12, 16, or however many that particular model boasts. The right side is where everything else happens: signal routing, effects importing, auxiliary inputs, master volume, monitor mixes, sub-mixing, headphone mixes, and other global functions. Even though the majority of the real estate is taken up by the left side, the right side is the one that requires the most intelligence to understand.

The Left Side—Top to Bottom

Though mixer controls are by no means standardized, most observe a certain top-to-bottom organization with respect to the order of the different controls. The graphic shows a typical mixer channel layout. Some models are fancier and have more regions or knobs per region, and some units are more basic and have fewer knobs, but this represents the basic scheme.

Trim

This controls the gain level of the preamp. For guitars, keyboards, and other line-level sources, you generally keep this control at or near the minimum (all the way to the left). For mics and piezo pickups, you'll need to crank it further to the right. The trim knob works in conjunction with the fader by "handicapping" signals so that differing input levels can be normalized, and then finely tuned with the faders.

EQ

The number of knobs and their functions will vary, but a common arrangement in lower- and mid-priced boards is to have four controls: high-shelving EQ, low-shelving EQ, and two midrange knobs that work in conjunction with each other. One selects the frequency and the other provides a boost or cut at that frequency. Many boards include a switch that bypasses EQ for signals requiring no board EQ.

Aux/Effects

Here is where you can send your signal out to external effects such as reverb, delay, flanger, and others. How far you crank the knob determines how much effect your signal gets. You can also use this level control to create a separate monitor mix, where the relative positions of all of the channels' aux send levels, and not the faders, determine the mix. A side note: You don't use this control on processors such as compressors, gates, and noise reducers. Those go "inline" with an instrument or through a channel's insert points.

Assign Switches

These switches route the signal to various *buses* or output paths. Typically, these are assigned in pairs and work in conjunction with the pan controls, where Tracks 1 and 2 are on one switch, Tracks 3 and 4 are on another, and so on. This way, any channel can be assigned to any track by choosing the appropriate switch (1/2, 3/4, etc.) and the correct odd/even pan assignment (odd=hard left, even=hard right).

Mute/Solo

These switches allow you to monitor any single instrument or a combination of instruments affecting the master mix. The mute switch kills the sound of a channel in the monitors. A solo switch kills every other sound but the one on that channel. These are invaluable tools when trying to correct a problem on the fly or in the context of a mix.

Fader

This is a level control that works in conjunction with the trim pot to control the overall strength of the signal. The optimal loudness should occur when the fader is at about 7/8 of its path. This point is usually indicated as 0 dB (i.e., no boost or cut) and is highlighted in some way for quick visual reference. If you're dealing with vastly different levels coming into the board—such as a powerful line level and a weak mic level—you should use the trim pot to normalize them first so that each signal is at equal loudness when their faders are at 0.

Channeling Your Energies

First, decide on your channel assignments. You might put a rhythm guitar on Channel 1, a bass on Channel 2, drums on Channels 3 and 4 (drums should be run in stereo, which requires two mixer channels panned hard right and hard left), and a lead guitar on Channel 5. Next, set up each instrument's channel in isolation. Adjust the trim, EQ, effect level, pan position, and overall loudness for each instrument, and listen to the results via your monitors or headphones. In my studio, I like to leave my channel assignments more-or-less permanent so that I don't have to turn every single knob from song to song or project to project. For example, I use only one lead vocal sound (and always with the same mic), so that channel remains fairly unchanged because the EQ is tailored to my voice. the level is adjusted to the type of mic, etc. This can help you to leave the left half—the big one—of the board as a "set and forget" situation. You'll be thankful for that when you get into the topsy-turvy world of the mixer's right half.

Mixer Logic—Part 2
Demystifying the Right Side of That Thing with All the Knobs
By Jon Chappell

In Part 1, I discussed the mixer's channel strips, which occupy the left side of the board. The right side is the *master section*, which consists of three main parts:

- Subgroup and master bus faders
- Auxiliary sends and returns
- Monitoring options

Different boards employ these features in different ways, but they all have a mastering section that's broken up into these three basic categories. First, I'll discuss the general features of each of these sections, and then look at the Mackie 1604 to show how a specific board is laid out according to this plan.

Subgroup and Master Bus Faders

The subgroup and master bus faders are where you route signals to tape, both for the multitrack machine (when tracking) and the two-track stereo machine (when mixing down). The fader at the furthest right is the master L/R bus fader. The master fader is usually used only in mix-down mode. When tracking, you use the subgroup faders immediately left of the master fader.

By pressing the assign switches and rotating the pan knob on the individual channels, you can route one or more signals to any subgroup bus. Most often, it is the subgroup outs that are connected to the tape inputs, while the master outputs are connected to the master mix-down deck. By having the channels first go to subgroups, you can, say, take seven channels of drums and group them to subgroup faders 1 and 2 (for left and right). Then you can preserve the relative mix of the drum set by raising and lowering only the two submaster faders, leaving the channel faders alone. You must also assign subgroup faders 1 to the main mix.

Auxiliary Sends and Returns

The aux section is where you bring in effects, any submixes (like a drum kit from another mixer), instruments that don't require a whole channel's worth of control (like synths, whose tonal and level changes can all be made on the instrument itself), or devices like CD players. Aux knobs determine how loud the auxiliary signals are going out of the board (*send*) and how loud the signals are going into the master bus (*return*). Use the aux send jack to find the best level for your processor (where the loudest channel aux send knob sends the input meter just slightly into the red) and use the master return to actually blend the desired mix of effected signal.

Monitoring Options

Engineers need to selectively listen to different aspects of the mix without affecting what goes on with either the musicians playing the music or the signal going to the multi-track. Making these audio inspections without disturbing the main mix is called *monitoring*. Typical things you would monitor are individual instruments (using the solo function), the subgroup buses (which might be used as monitor mixes for the musicians), the effects bus, and any signal that you would want on the final mix, but not in the musicians' headphones (such as a voice-over or narration).

Let's take a look at how the Mackie 1604-VLZ Pro lays out the three categories of bus faders, aux signals, and monitoring. See the diagram and the captions for a breakdown of the 1604's right side.

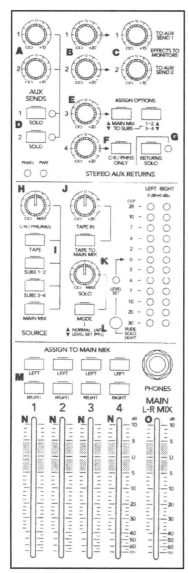

The right side, or master section, of the Mackie 1604-VLZ Pro

Aux

A—Volume controls for aux sends 1 and 2

B—Volume controls for aux returns 1 and 2

C—Effect levels for aux 1 and 2

D—Solo buttons (to listen to just aux 1 and/or 2)

E—Aux 3 and 4 level controls, plus switches that enable you to route their stereo return buses to subgroups 1/2 or 3/4. This allows the effect to be reduced along with the straight signal.

F—C-R/PHNS switch: Removes Aux 4's signal from the main mix and sends it to monitors (active only in solo mode)

G—Returns solo switch: Allows you to hear just the effects (this way you can hear any channels that are soloed plus their effects)

Monitoring

H—Volume for control room speakers or headphones

I—Switches to select tape (or CD) player, subgroups 1/2 and/or 3/4, and the main (L/R) mix

J—Volume for tape (or CD) player signal; switch to place tape into main (L/R) mix

K—Solo mode: Normal/AFL (After Fade Listen) reflects fader position, Level Set/PFL (Pre Fade Listen) is unaffected by the volume faders' position (*Level Set* refers to Mackie's suggested procedure for setting proper input levels)

L—Rude solo light: Lets you know when you've accidentally engaged a solo button and saves you from losing your mind trying to find "the problem," which is especially vexing when you've soloed an unused or silent channel

Buses

M—Assign switches: Determine whether subgroup buses are assigned to the left and/or right main mix, or not at all (as in the case of a separate cue mix for musicians)

N—Subgroup faders: Control the volume levels for all of the instruments assigned to these buses (determined by the bus assign switch and pan knob in the channel strip section)

O—Main mix fader: Determines the volume level of everything assigned to the main mix, including subgroup buses and auxiliary signals

Desktop Mixing
Your Digital Audio Workstation Console
By David Darlington

Most of us have seen or toyed with the mixer window in our sequencer or audio software, but can software simulation really substitute for a hardware desk? The answer is a resounding "Yes!" but only if you know how to use it properly. Let's have a look at how software mixers resemble their stand-alone cousins and how they differ.

There are three types of sound input channels: MIDI, audio, and audio instrument (software synth). Each MIDI track is represented by a fader that controls its level. When you move the fader, it sends a MIDI volume message to the sound module that corresponds to the fader. Audio tracks are handled similarly, with the fader controlling the output from the audio card for that audio voice. The third type of input is the audio instrument, or *soft synth*. Most of these use the CPU to generate sound, and then route this sound through the audio card. In this case, the fader controls level through the audio card. Some soft synths have their own cards, such as Digidesign's SampleCell, and the mixer's fader then controls the output of the dedicated cards. Software faders aren't designed to emulate their hardware cousins. They have an input—either MIDI or audio—and an output, and usually feature a number of auxiliary sends and insert points. The sends are paths by which you can route the sound to places other than the mix output. The insert points are used to access software plug-ins that process the sound. Insert points can also be assigned to your audio card's inputs and outputs to route an outboard processor to the audio track. Stereo faders also feature a panning knob. All of this information can be automated using your audio sequencer.

Most software mixers offer auxiliary faders that can be used in a number of ways. I find that these extra routing paths confuse many musicians, but they can be very helpful in organizing your mix. One good use is to open a stereo aux fader and assign a stereo bus to its input. Now, an audio signal with its output assigned to this bus will pass through the aux fader on its way out to the mix. This is a great way to control the level of multiple tracks like backing vocals, percussion, and drums. You can use EQ, compression, or any other plug-in as an insert on the aux fader and thereby affect the entire group of tracks.

Another use of the aux fader is as an effect return. Assign a stereo bus to the input of a stereo aux track and insert an effect plug-in such as reverb or delay into the insert path of the aux fader. Assign the sends of your audio channels to this same bus to add reverb to the sound. Using reverb as an insert in one audio fader wastes a lot of computing power on one sound. Applying reverb via the aux fader allows many sounds to use the same reverb.

The last type of fader you'll find on your desktop is called a *master fader*. Unlike hardware mixers, software mixers can have more than one master—in fact, they can support a master fader for each output of your audio hardware. The most common use of a master fader is on audio outputs 1 and 2 (i.e., the L/R output of your mix) to add final compression or EQ to the overall mix.

Use the software mixer to both maximize the power contained in your software and minimize the strain on your computer's CPU. You'll find that an understanding of the subtleties of the desktop mixer can open up a whole new world of creativity.

Organizing Your Mix
Clear the Way for a Clean Result
By David Darlington

Sometimes the hardest part of a task is just rolling up your sleeves and getting started. Certainly, mixing a song can be a daunting challenge, simply because it implies commitment and finality. You must decide how things will sound and then follow through for better or worse. If you prepare the track and mixer layout intelligently, get your outboard tools in order so you can access them quickly, and get rid of all of the unused extraneous elements, you can concentrate on the task at hand and maintain a clear train of thought all the way to the finish line. Here are a few tips on how to tidy up your layout and work efficiently when approaching the all-important final mix.

First, it's helpful visually to group similar types of instruments together, regardless of the order in which they were recorded. For example, assign the drums to the far left of the mixer, starting with the kick and assigning each drum track to the adjacent channels. Follow drum kit tracks with loops and percussion sounds. Then add bass tracks, keyboards, guitars, and vocals (backing vocals, lead vocals, and then solos). Now your mix is laid out from left to right, representing the sound spectrum loosely from low frequency to high and, musically, from the foundation of the rhythm section to the icing on the cake—the solos.

If your mixer has edit groups, you can assign families of instruments to their own group. Try setting drums to one group and percussion to another so that they can be muted or raised and lowered as a whole in the mix. To adjust individual levels within the group, just disable the group temporarily. In a software mixer, you can use auxiliary faders as group masters to apply EQ or compression to a whole group at once. Often, compressing the drums or brightening the percussion group really helps the overall mix. Also, since members of the same instrument family are usually near each other, it's easy to assess relative levels, panning, and EQs. For example, if all of the hi-hats and shakers are grouped together, it's easy to check that they are panned away from each other and not fighting within the mix. Also, when you are working on other parts and you realize one shaker is too loud, you won't have to scour a long track list to find it.

Another good way to prepare is to set up auxiliary sends and effect returns before you get started. You'll need at least one reverb, probably two, and a few delays are always helpful. I generally set up two stereo returns for reverb and two mono returns for delay while I'm organizing my tracks. Of course, you should tailor these settings to your mix as you work, but at least you won't have to interrupt your flow just to put a little delay on something. If you're working with a software mixer, dedicate Send A *globally* (i.e., on every fader) to the first reverb, Send B to the second, and so on. This way, you won't have to slow down to hear reverb on a channel since the send is already in place and so is the return. If you have a channel strip–type plug-in, you might want to assign it globally to Insert A so that EQ and compression are also readily available. This is only a good idea if your digital audio workstation has enough power to create that many plug-ins; otherwise, just insert when necessary.

Finally, clear away the clutter. There are always a few tracks lying around that probably won't be used in the final mix (maybe the bagpipe solo wasn't such a good idea after all). Believe me, I understand track separation anxiety—but really, let it go. Save the file as a separate "mix" session and delete all of the unnecessary tracks. They will still exist in the old file and can be pulled in if necessary. This goes for vocal outtakes, scratch tracks, and unused doubling. Less clutter enables you to work more efficiently, and your mixes will take much less time. Less distraction for your eyes and brain will enable you to better use your most important resource—your ears.

Active Listening
How to Avoid Getting Lost in the Details on Your Way to a Great Mix
By Pat Kirtley

Most of the time—say, 99 percent of it—we use our senses in a passive way. We see and hear without ever thinking about the process. Even when we concentrate on something such as watching a TV screen—ignoring everything else in our field of vision—the focusing happens on an automatic, subconscious level.

There are times, though, when you become consciously aware of what the sensory systems are doing, such as when you're trying to feel with your fingertips in the dark to find which key belongs to your front door, or visually examining a piece of art to determine how the painter applied his brushstrokes. At those times, you are thinking while you are sensing, and you direct your senses. In the realm of recording and mixing, the ability to direct your listening attention, also called *active listening,* is one of the most useful—and necessary—skills.

Here are some secrets well known to the top mixing pros, and some exercises you can use to take your own recording and mixing chops to the next level.

Overall Listening Level

Back in the 1940s, some researchers discovered that the *tonal balance* of human hearing—how much bass vs. how much treble you can hear—is affected in a very precise way by the overall level of the sound source. They also found that the frequency response of the ear is never *flat*—like a straight-line graph—at any listening level. The significant thing they discovered as regards mixing engineers is that, at low listening levels, the ear's bass response drops off drastically; the treble-end response goes down too, but to a lesser degree. As the overall volume is raised, the frequency response of hearing becomes more uniform until it becomes almost flat at high levels of intensity, The "loudness" or "bass boost" button found on virtually every piece of audio amplifying equipment was put there in an effort to counteract the loss of bass response at low listening levels.

How do you use this human hearing factor to your advantage in recording and mixing? A group of mix engineers decided some years back to standardize the average listening level in control rooms to one that would be high enough to overcome most of the frequency response curve losses, but low enough to avoid long-term hearing damage and listening fatigue. They decided on a sound level of 85 decibels, on the *A weighted measurement scale.*

You can buy an inexpensive sound level measuring meter and easily calibrate your own home studio monitoring level. Even if you don't understand all of the scientific "whys" of using this method, your mixes will immediately benefit from it.

Accommodation

Sensory researchers use the term *accommodation* to express the idea of the senses getting used to something. Our senses have developed over the millennia to accommodate a number of conditions—bright sunlight, near total darkness, someone whispering, the sound of a roaring river—by opening up or closing down to compensate for the amount of incoming sensory information.

If you have attended rock concerts, you have probably experienced this strange effect: The music seems to be too loud at first, after a while it seems okay, but then you go outside after the concert is over and you can't even tell what the person next to you is saying when he speaks with his usual volume levels. What happens is that your hearing system shuts itself down by constricting muscles inside the ear to physically reduce the sensitivity of the eardrum. This is the most drastic example of auditory accommodation, but it is important to learn that there are more moderate forms of this action that affect our hearing all of the time.

The most common accommodation effect is when the hearing process automatically tunes out sounds it thinks that you don't need to hear (i.e., putting them further away in your consciousness), and focuses on the things it thinks you do need to hear (i.e., bringing them forward into your active attention). For example, as you listen to music while you work at your DAW, your hearing tends to involuntarily "straighten out" the levels and tonal balance to make it sound better! A shrill mid-range peak in a singer's voice is gradually smoothed away so that at some point before the first cut is over, your ear is no longer distracted by the problem. In casual listening situations this is fine, but in the case of mixing it's a potential productivity killer.

You want to make a mix that will stand the test of time and conform reasonably to the current standards of tonal and level balance. Yet every time you start mixing, your hearing adjusts so that what you think you heard ten minutes ago now sounds very different—and you don't know why. If you don't realize what the accommodation phenomenon is doing to your hearing, you usually end up frustrated. The mix you thought sounded so great at the end of the session two days ago now sounds like a hopeless mess.

To get away from the tyranny of auditory accommodation, first you must be aware that it's *always* happening. You can't hear it changing, but you can keep reminding yourself that it is. The longer you listen to a mix, the more drastic the accommodation. You can get back to reality by listening at intervals to a good mix from a CD you like and respect. If the overall sound of your work is seriously deviating from this reference, it will be obvious and you can make positive corrections. Another important thing is to take breaks at regular intervals (at least ten to 15 minutes every hour) to allow your hearing to return to normal.

Even when using the techniques above, after many hours of listening you will be under the influence of a further auditory problem—*listening fatigue*—and your capacity for critical judgment will be greatly diminished. With tired ears, nothing is going to sound right. The recovery time for listening fatigue is a few hours at least, but an overnight rest is best.

Active Focus

The ears have an uncanny ability to zero in on fine details within a dense mix of sound. With enough concentration, you can begin to hear strange little things—buzzes and rattles in the bass guitar strings, a squeaky foot pedal on the hi-hat stand, or a strange pinging echo sound in the reverb. Most of these things pass right by the ears of the casual listener, but as you listen to the same tune again and again in mixing or tracking, those weird little items can get louder and louder. If you are also a musician who is performing on the recording (as is so often the case with home project studios), you may begin to focus in on tiny playing fluffs and intonations. It can drive you crazy.

This micro-attention to detail can be counterproductive. You must learn to actively direct the point of focus. While you are learning how to do it, you will fight against long-established inner mechanisms whose job is to even things out. When you first realize that you are hearing tiny details you never noticed before, it's really a good thing—it shows that you have made the first step toward critical, active listening. The next step is to control this focus.

Concentrate on Level Balances

Many aspects of the sounds you hear while mixing are randomly competing for your attention. Your task as an active listener is to focus on the important aspects first. A good way to simplify this task is to think in a most basic way—to mix by adjusting levels only. Eventually, there are many other things that you must address to get a killer mix, but for the sake of training your ears, imagine that you have only level faders to work with and that the rest of your electronic arsenal—even simple EQ—doesn't exist.

Now, you can experiment with mixing only by level balances between the instruments and voices. In the past, many consoles were designed so that in the mode where tracks were being played back during overdubbing, the monitor mix was affected only by level controls and nothing else.

Even in this radically simplified scenario, your hearing wants to play some funny tricks. The first is due to the illusion we call "stereo." Some sound engineers have called our current system "two-speaker mono," and they have good reasons for their skepticism. The two-speaker mode of listening is an attempt to create a wider field of sound, and to some degree it works. In the multitrack production of popular music, various tracks are assigned "positions" (hard left, hard right, and anywhere in between) in the stereo field via the panning controls.

The stereo mix/listening problem stems largely from the fact that a great amount of effort has been spent to get a reasonably good stereo image in control room and monitoring setups, but in the real world, the final listener will probably have a lousy stereo image or perhaps none at all. My favorite example is the typical stereo in a car—where no listener gets a good left-right balance but a great deal of consumer listening is done. Almost no one listens to music the way engineers do in the mixing room.

In the studio, there is an unrealistically wonderful listening environment that bathes the ears in the seductive wash of the stereo field. Our ears are pulled in by an aspect that is largely absent for most listeners. You must learn to concentrate on the mix—not the stereo—and some consoles offer you an easy way to do this. It's called the *mono button*. When you press it, the same sound goes to both speakers. The relative spatial position doesn't affect your attention now, but relative levels sure do.

Even better than using the mono button is to begin your mix with all of the pan pots set to their center positions. You can make a good mix in mono and then do the panning assignments afterwards. Yes, the sound picture will become more interesting and colorful when you spread things out, but your mixing decisions will not have been based on stereo prettiness and will hold up in many different listening environments.

Time Is Not on Our Side

Mixing music is a frustrating exercise when you're trying to change something after it has already happened. We make changes, rewind, and then listen to a passage repeatedly to fine-tune the result. Eventually, this disjointed process of repeatedly listening to bits and pieces of music begins to have an affect on the brain of you, the mixing engineer. You begin listening to very precise aspects of the sound, sometimes focusing on disconnected snippets of time. The more you do this, the further you drift from the big picture—the whole mix as the listener will experience it.

The trick here is to distance yourself from the mix at regular intervals. Resting your ears and coming back the next day is always a good idea, but there are other ways to get a fresh perspective. My favorite distancing technique is to get up while the mix is playing, leave the room, close the door, and listen. All of the in-your-face directness and decoration of the mix is then blocked out. What's left? The good part. If the music still sounds reasonable—with good balances between all of the instruments and vocals—you've probably got it right. If not, you'll immediately know what to correct.

It's All Relative

Keep in mind that any single aspect of a mix that has your direct attention will sound louder than the rest of the mix. When you work on the relative levels, it is this that causes the most errors. So, when you are adjusting one particular level in the context of the band mix, direct your mind *away* from that track to the whole mix and then back again.

Always keep in mind how the listener will experience the final work. When all is done with the mix, put it away for a day or so, and then come back to listen again, but this time try to put on the mindset of your potential listener. What do they want to hear? Are they concentrating on the vocals at that point or the song as a whole? It is surprising what insights this change of reference can give you.

When recording and mixing, always be aware that your hearing system is a better tool than any piece of gear in your arsenal. If you apply some effort to consciously override your unconscious perceptions and learn from the experience of doing so, you are on your way to being one of those recordists who can *really* get it right.

Soundcheck Before You Mix

As you begin each mixing session:

- Set the room listening level to approximately 85 dB (use a sound level meter set to the "A weighted" mode).

- Make sure that there are no tone-affecting settings in your monitoring system. Turn the loudness control off and set all EQ in the monitor chain flat.

- Before you begin mixing your materials, listen to a couple of known good mixes that you like in order to get a feel for the room level and get used to reasonable tonal balances.

- Assemble a rough mix without worrying about effects, stereo spread, or EQ changes. Work for good relative mix levels *only*. If the mix is a band with vocals, do the band first and then add the vocals.

- Remember that relative level balances are crucial—everything else is decoration.

A Checklist for Intelligent Mixing

- Always be conscious that your ears are the main tools in your mixing arsenal. Be equally conscious that they can become unreliable for a number of reasons, and that you must be actively in control of them. This is the hardest part of learning to be a good mix engineer, but it is what separates the professionals from the novices.

- When you encounter a mix that sounds balanced one moment and unbalanced the next, consider using compression on the problem track(s). Apply overall compression to the stereo mix only after you have achieved a good balance.

- Listen through different speakers and with different levels of attention. Listen in mono. Listen from out in the hallway with the door closed. A well-balanced mix will sound good even in these compromised situations.

- Use EQ to solve mixing problems, not to add decoration. This rule may be creatively broken, but it is a good guideline to use while you are learning.

- The listener's auditory accommodation will mentally adjust for EQ variances in your mixes, but it cannot improve level imbalances. Mix for levels—always.

- Remember that all of the sounds in your mix are full-range sources. A bass sound can have lots of high-frequency aspects and a ride cymbal can have strong lows. Stop thinking of sounds as being "bass" or "treble." Mix levels, not tones.

- Be prepared to rethink your mix the next day or the next week. Your best mixing judgments are usually made early in a session, when your mind is alert and your ears are not fatigued. Stretch your useful mixing day by taking regular "ear breaks."

- Learn by listening to great mixes as if they were your own. Listen to a recording you enjoy and respect through your monitor system; sit in front of the mixer and imagine you just finished putting it together. It's a great psychological exercise, and what you can hear when you listen this way may surprise you.

A CD Mastering Primer
Preparing Your Disc for the Duplicator
By Pat Kirtley

Okay, I know I've said previously that you should never try to master your own CDs—that you should spend some bucks and benefit from the experience of professional mastering engineers. But then you just wouldn't listen, would you? You've been slyly burning your own masters while you thought no one was looking. Well, I've heard some of them and, boy, does my original advice still apply—but you're probably not going to quit doing it. You're gonna keep jamming audio digits onto discs in the hopes of someday getting it right, aren't you? So, admitting the obvious, I'm going to break down here and teach you some mastering basics so your discs won't be so—well, lame.

Here is a primer on mastering for people who should know better than to try it. I won't use too many complex terms, and I will assume that you have some sort of CD burner (a stand-alone unit or computer CD-R drive) and that you know how to send it your audio signals.

Any mastering engineer will tell you that the task of CD mastering can fall into one of two categories: trying to preserve beautiful mixes or salvage awful ones. The top mastering guys see more of the former, but as an amateur recordist you will encounter a fair amount of the latter. But it's good to see problems when you are in a learning mode and, by knowing what does and doesn't work at the mastering stage, you will also learn how to do mixes that are more compatible with the "real world."

Mastering has two main objectives: to take a collection of recorded cuts and put them together so that they flow as a unified work, and to allow these cuts to best utilize the available dynamic range of the recording system. Secondary tasks in mastering concern what you might call detail work—things such as fade-outs and spacing between tunes.

Mastering also offers a "second chance" for a problem mix. The mastering engineer affords the artist and producer another set of ears through which to reconsider some of the decisions made during mixing. Now, you're thinking, "But what if the artist, producer, and mastering engineer are all the same person?" Good question, and therein lies one of the big problems with mastering your own projects. However, by putting yourself into "mastering mode," and keeping your various roles and tasks separate in your mind, you can begin to gain the necessary objectivity.

In mastering, there isn't much room for guesswork, and it's the reason mastering engineers are a special breed—the "perfectionists" of the recording engineer world. One of the first things mastering engineers learn is limits—how big, fat, loud, or soft sounds can be on the disc and still play back properly on a multitude of systems out in the consumer world. Overall, mastering engineers tend to be a conservative bunch. Their approach is not unlike the creed every physician learns in medical school: *First, do no harm*. If you learn nothing else about mastering, knowing that the mastering process must preserve and not degrade audio signals will serve you well.

Speaking of learning, I feel obligated to make a disclaimer here. CD mastering is an intrinsic part of the commercial record-making process. It has evolved through painstaking development, and doing it well requires people with years of experience and specialized rooms filled with sophisticated gear. There are no shortcuts to making great records. You, as a novice mastering person, are at the bottom end of a steep learning curve. The most useful decisions you will make while cutting your own master discs will be basic ones, based more on common sense than on technical experience—experience that you can't get from a book or a primer article like this one.

So, before rushing out and spending a lot of money for mastering tools of either the hardware or software variety, consider that your "masters" will probably be more suited for demos than retail or radio-ready commercial products. When the time comes to put out a real commercial product, your money will be better spent on the services of a professional mastering service.

In the meantime, you can achieve very decent, if basic, CD masters by intelligently utilizing features and tools that are built into nearly every computer-based editing suite or all-in-one multitrack recording and mixing system. Probably the worst mastering fiascoes I've heard have come from people who thought that they could purchase some high-rated does-everything box, run the audio through it, and presto—it would sound like their favorite artist. Yeah, right—and if I buy the right camera, my pictures will look just like those of Ansel Adams. You will be better served to approach the mastering realm with a sense of humility, and a realization that learning can be its own joy.

What Is a Master?

A *master disc* is one that is used for reproducing discs or other media. In a way, it is like a photographic negative that will be used to make many final prints. It must be nearly perfect in many technical aspects, or there will be problems during later duplication and reproduction on consumer playback systems. Besides the obvious audio signal carried in digital form within the CD signal stream, there is also control data in the form of timing and start and end signals that must be properly recorded into the data as the CD is created. In mastering, you can't assume all of this will happen automatically, and you need to understand these hidden aspects if you are going to avoid duplication and playback problems.

Not too many years ago, the preferred media for CD mastering—i.e., the media you send to the disc manufacturing plant—was either DAT or a larger type of tape called a 1630 U-Matic cassette, which used 3/4" wide tape originally designed for video, not audio. Now, most CD masters are submitted in the form of a CD-R. Using a CD-R disc eliminates a lot of potential shortcomings of the DAT and 1630 media types, and instead of purchasing (or renting) a $1,000 DAT machine, you can use the same CD-R drive found in almost all new computers or a sub-$500 stand-alone CD recorder. One major advantage of using CD-Rs as CD masters is that you can play back the master on any CD player for verification and allow yourself to hear how the product sounds in different playback environments.

Methodology

There are several methods for making CD-Rs, including those involving computer-based systems and dedicated stand-alone CD recorder units. With either type of system, you end up with the same CD master, but there are differences in the capabilities each offers.

Computer-based systems (either a PC/Mac with an attached CD-R drive, or a digital multitrack machine with an optional CD-R system) have the advantage of more precise control. Through software, you can specify many parameters and set it all up ahead of time.

With a dedicated CD-R deck, the options are fewer, and many decks force you to make CDs with, for instance, a specific gap time between tracks so that you can't create a seamless blend between two sequential cuts. With most stand-alone decks, you must have the set of tracks to be recorded already set up and in exact order on a separate machine.

However, the stand-alone decks have one strong asset that is difficult or nonexistent on the computer-based systems: They can accept analog input (e.g., from a reel-to-reel tape machine or radio broadcast) and burn a CD from it in real time. On computer-based systems, you must first dump all of the audio onto a hard disk and then use that stored data to make CD copies.

Peak Levels, Density, and Rogue Peaks

The topic of "levels" in mastering is the basis of many heated discussions, with widely differing opinions from highly qualified engineers. However, the basic concepts are not complicated. We can look at the concept of levels in several different ways.

The first is the *absolute level*. In digital audio, a program's highest and lowest levels are governed by simple mathematics—there are absolute limits that cannot be exceeded. Digital CD audio encodes each sample of a sound recording into numbers ranging from 0 to 65,000. The top level, the mathematical "65,000," shows up on the audio metering side as "0 dB." All levels lower than this are prefaced by a minus sign. The lowest possible level, mathematical zero (0), is translated to an audio meter reading of approximately −96 decibels. Within this range of highest to lowest, all CD audio reproduction takes place.

Each track or selection you prepare to place on the master CD will have a highest peak level of so many decibels, expressed as a minus number referenced to the unsurpassable 0 dB. It is quite likely that each track will have a different maximum peak level. One of the goals of mastering is to get a consistent audio level over the whole CD so that the ear doesn't perceive a drastic difference between cuts. It would be nice if achieving this consistency was a matter of scaling (or normalizing) each track's volume so that maximum level was the same for each track. Sadly, it's not that easy.

The maximum peak that occurs in a given recorded track may be one that is extraordinarily higher than the average level of the music—a *rogue peak*. The intensity of this short burst of energy often will have nothing to do with the musical content. These errant peaks are sometimes caused by things like popped "p" consonants uttered by singers, or string squeaks from close-miked acoustic guitars. They may not sound as loud as the meter reading would indicate—and consequently reducing their energy does not make the music sound any different.

So what's the problem? Well, these rogue peaks can cause overloads and potential distortion in playback systems. They also limit how high the overall level of the track can be taken, since the digital maximum level (0 dB) is an unsurpassable limit. How do you deal with this?

First, you locate the rogue peaks. If you are using a computer with editing software and a waveform monitor, you have the best means to deal with this issue. You may see a few peaks standing much higher than the surrounding audio terrain. Go to each one, listen to it, and then highlight just the peak and reduce its volume; peaks of shorter time durations can be reduced more easily than broader ones. Next, play back the section(s) to make sure that the change doesn't create any audible anomalies.

If the peak were truly a wild deviation of nonmusical content, you would hear little or no difference. What you have done, though, by reducing the peak level at this instant is to raise the overall average level of the recording. In the case of very "peaky" material, raising the average is the only way to get some tracks up to a level where they sound consistent with the others in a group. Once you have managed to get the extreme peaks under control, you can then raise the overall level of the track, using a function called normalization.

The Ups and Downs of Normalization

Normalization is a digital audio function that simply finds the highest peak in a musical selection, calls it "0 dB," and scales the level of the entire selection upward according to this peak. It's a two-step process—one pass to find the highest peak and measure its level, and then a second pass to scale the level of the entire selection accordingly. In terms of what goes on computation-wise, it is a straightforward process. On some software systems, you can choose to normalize to a level less than 0 dB; for instance, you can set a maximum level of –2 dB. But what good is normalization?

First of all, it's useful if only for bringing the levels up on recordings that are weak. You do not normalize downward; if a recording has already been overloaded on high peaks, there is no way to undo that problem. Also, using normalization to make a recorded selection sound louder is usually pointless, too; raising a level 4 dB by normalization, for instance, looks drastic on the computer screen, but the results sound only somewhat louder. Normalization is pretty much a function for getting all of your recordings in the same ballpark for levels—that's all.

All Bits Are Off: Digital Silence

Between each cut on a digital final master, there is a silent period of typically one to three seconds. The specification says that this is *digital silence*, which means that it is a section of digital code consisting of "all zeros." Inserting a digital silence period is pretty easy with computer-based systems—the CD-burning software can automatically insert it for you between cuts. Basic software sometimes uses a default two-second time, but with more sophisticated software you can specify the silence between each cut.

However, with a stand-alone CD recorder, creating these silences is more difficult. If your connection with the playback machine or computer containing your collection of cuts is going into the CD recorder through an analog connection (i.e., left and right line input jacks), there is no "digital" silence between the cuts. Even though you hear nothing while listening at these spots, the signal will not go to true digital all-zeroes. Problems can arise, including the inability of the CD recorder to automatically create a new track number for each cut. If the machine has a mute button on the input, you can press it at the appropriate time to insert silence and cause the machine to step to the next track number. Some machines can intelligently sense near-silence and then automatically create a new track.

But all of this can be tricky. It is much better to connect a playback recorder (or computer) to a CD recorder using a digital connection (fiber optic or hardwired connection). Digital silences between tracks will then be transferred and acted upon correctly.

Beyond the technical aspects of inter-track silences, you can creatively use this gap time to make the music flow better. If a loud piece that ends with a flourish is to be followed by a soft ballad, extra time allows the listener's ears to settle down for the much quieter beginning of the new piece. Conversely, at the end of a piece that features a long and languorous 20-second fade-out, you may want to make the gap time as short as possible leading into the next piece. If you have CD-burning software that automatically inserts a fixed two-second or so gap time, you can insert silent periods at the beginning or ending of cuts via editing software, or by using a very old-fashioned method: pausing the playback machine.

Sweetening

Mastering engineers use the term *sweetening* to describe changes applied during the mastering process that are based on subjective opinions and preferences. Subjective implies that what is sweet to one person's ears might be obnoxious to others. Typically, sweetening involves adjusting equalization and adding reverb or other effects at mastering time. EQ is routinely applied at mastering time, but usually in quantities that are much less than what you might use during mixing.

Remember that EQ applied to a two-track master affects every sound on a recording at once—you can't enhance just one thing. The best and gentlest approach to mastering EQ is to make adjustments only at the ends of the spectrum—i.e., below 200 Hz and above about 5,000 Hz. If you restrict yourself to just these ranges, you will be surprised at how much of an overall difference in balance they can make. Most problems involving EQ imbalances between cuts on a CD can be fixed with small alterations in these ranges.

Adding reverb is even trickier. The good thing is that you can experiment easily with different reverb characteristics and amounts to find something that is compatible with the program material and truly enhances the mix. Again, remember: The reverb you apply at mastering time affects everything in the mix, and low-frequency–heavy sources such as kick drums and basses don't take added reverb well. If you need to add reverb and don't want to affect the bottom end of things, you can experiment with EQing the reverb itself.

It's always a good idea not to make indelible changes to the one and only copy of your master mix. You can always burn a CD of your material prior to any mastering changes as a safety measure. That way, if you go too far off the deep end with processing, or make some huge mistake and then save the file, you can always go back to a known starting point. The pros wouldn't do it any other way.

Burning Issues and Quality Control

When it's time to actually burn the CD master, you should use as much care as the guys in the professional mastering studios do. It's a matter of close attention to detail, as well as knowing about some of the common problems to look out for.

CD drives installed in personal computers sometimes have problems making audio CDs. Remember that these devices are designed to work in a number of different types of computers, and the drive manufacturer cannot know what other hardware or software is installed on a given computer. None of this technology was ever designed to be an audio mastering system; the CD-ROM is primarily a straight digital storage medium, and audio capabilities on computer drives are sort of a glorious afterthought.

The types of problems you may encounter include gaps in the recording, and sections of a track missing with no audible gap (as if something were removed by an editing process). To minimize potential problems, treat the computer during the CD writing phase as if CD mastering were its only job.

Do a clean start-up or reboot, and run the CD mastering program all by itself. Disable all automatic "reminder" programs (alarms, virus checkers, etc.), and network and internet connections, and turn off screen savers that trigger after a certain period of inactivity. These programs can steal needed processor cycles at critical moments during the CD writing process and cause digital hiccups that you can hear in the final product. It's crucial to have enough memory in the computer to accommodate the process, too. To that end, you should not have other programs loaded during the writing phase. Even if the other programs are "minimized," they take up valuable memory space.

None of these PC-based conflicts exist in dedicated audio CD-writing decks, but quality problems with CD blanks can occur with either type of system. This is why you must listen critically to any disc you make that will be designated as a replication master—any defect, no matter how small, will be faithfully reproduced across hundreds or even thousands of final product discs.

Listen to the master disc on a good quality deck, listen with headphones so that you can micro-focus, and try not to listen to the music at all. Instead listen for funny little problems "around the edges"—clicks, pops, tics, and gaps. It can be difficult to hear these small artifacts because you get used to hearing the music from earlier mixing and listening sessions and your brain sometimes fills in the gaps, masking out problems. But at some point, someone will hear these artifacts if they are present and call them to your attention. The funny thing is, once you hear a problem, it never goes away, so be sure to check ever so carefully to ensure a clean master disc.

And Finally—Finalizing

When CD-R discs are recorded, there are many ways that the data might be used. In the case of *Red Book audio*, which is the format we use to make CD masters, the disc must be *finalized* in order to be able to play back on any CD player. This process writes some extra information on the disc that tells a CD player what kind of disc it is, and where the tracks are located. In computer software, finalizing can involve simply checking a box on the screen prior to burning the CD; on stand-alone recorders, it is generally a matter of pressing a button on the front panel. Just remember to do it.

Now you are ready to begin making better CD master discs. If you develop an attitude that your main tasks are to tidy up and preserve the quality of recordings and mixes, to get a good balance from track to track, and always to stay away from extremes of processing, you'll do just fine.

Coaster Avoidance—Tips for Burning the Perfect CD Master

It's not such a tragedy as it once was to make a bad CD-R. When discs used to cost upwards of $15 each, turning out an accidental "coaster" was sure to produce a stream of expletives. Now discs are dirt cheap and CD-R drives have improved dramatically—but care and quality control are still important. A problematic disc sent away as a production master can cost you dearly in time and dollars. So, here are a few hints to avoid headaches.

Use quality CD-R master discs. Some engineers say that there are fewer data errors with the lighter-colored gold and silver discs than with the dark green or dark blue ones.

Handle the disc carefully by the edges when transferring it from the package to the CD drive. Even small specks of dust can cause write errors, and if you accidentally get a fingerprint on the active surface, you might as well toss the disc and get another one. Think "laboratory clean."

Skip the nice-looking paper labels that many people like to use on CD-Rs. They can cause all kinds of problems down the road, including data-read errors if they cause the disc to get just slightly out of balance. Use a permanent marking pen (or pens specially designed for writing on discs) for labeling right on the disc surface.

If possible, forgo the "8X," "6X," and other fast writing speeds and burn your master at "1X" speed to reduce possible errors (okay—you can use 2X if you are really impatient).

What You Can and Can't Fix in Mastering

You can:

- Adjust relative levels between cuts
- Create a smooth fade-out at the end of a track
- Add reverb or other effects to the whole track
- Use compression (very carefully!) to raise the average level of a track
- Use equalization to adjust the overall tonal balance of a track
- Adjust the silent time between cuts to create the best overall flow

You can't:

- Undo distortion caused by overdriven levels
- Change balances between sound sources in the mix
- Remove excessive reverb or effects
- Make a bad recording sound good

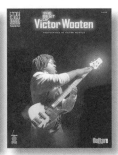